CRIMINAL JUSTICE

IN NORTH CAROLINA

ELLEN G. COHN

Florida International University

Upper Saddle River, New Jersey 07458

Publisher: Stephen Helba
Executive Editor: Frank Mortimer, Jr.
Assistant Editor: Sara Holle
Production Editor: Barbara Cappuccio
Director of Manufacturing and Production: Bruce Johnson
Managing Editor: Mary Carnis
Manufacturing Buyer: Cathleen Petersen
Creative Director: Cheryl Asherman
Cover Design Coordinator: Miguel Ortiz
Cover Design: Denise Brown
Cover Image: Day Williams/Photo Researchers, Inc.

Pearson Prentice Hall™ is a trademark of Pearson Education, Inc.
Pearson® is a registered trademark of Pearson plc
Prentice Hall® is a registered trademark of Pearson Education, Inc.

Pearson Education LTD.
Pearson Education Singapore, Pte. Ltd
Pearson Education, Canada, Ltd
Pearson Education–Japan
Pearson Education Australia PTY, Limited
Pearson Education North Asia Ltd
Pearson Educaçion de Mexico, S.A. de C.V.
Pearson Education Malaysia, Pte. Ltd

10 9 8 7 6 5 4 3
ISBN 0-13-114030-2

CONTENTS

PREFACE

This supplementary text will provide you with specific information on the North Carolina criminal law and the North Carolina criminal justice system. Throughout the text, you will find quotations which have been taken verbatim from legal documents, such as the North Carolina General Statutes and the North Carolina State Constitution. Any misspellings or other irregularities are reproduced exactly as they appear in the original documents.

I hope that you enjoy this supplement and find it both interesting and informative. If you have any questions, comments, or suggestions, please feel free to contact me via email.

Ellen G. Cohn, Ph.D.
cohne@fiu.edu

CHAPTER 1

THE STATE OF NORTH CAROLINA

INTRODUCTION

North Carolina is located in the southeastern portion of the United States, and is bounded by Virginia on the North, South Carolina and Georgia on the south, Tennessee on the west, and the Atlantic Ocean on the east. It was one of the original thirteen colonies and is believed to be the first to declare independence from Great Britain. The state bird is the cardinal, the state flower is the dogwood, the state insect is the honey bee, and the state tree is the southern pine. The capital of North Carolina is Raleigh but the largest city is Charlotte. State nicknames include the 'Tar Heel State" and the "Old North State."

THE HISTORY OF NORTH CAROLINA

North Carolina in the 16th Century

The early Native American population of North Carolina appears to have included about 30 different tribes, divided into three main linguistic groups. The Iroquoian tribes included the Cherokee, Coree, and Tuscarora. They were found primarily in the western portion of the state and on the coastal plains. The Siouan tribes included Catawba, Eno, Tutelo, Saponi, and Cheraw and were mainly located in the central area of the state. The Algonquian tribes, which were found in the tidewater region, included the Hatteras, Pamlico, Chowan, and Secotan. By the mid-1600s, the population of Native Americans in the region was estimated to be about 30,000 in total.

The first European to visit North Carolina was Giovanni da Verrazzano, a Florentine who led a French expedition to the region in 1524. He explored the coastal area between Kitty Hawk and Cape Fear River. The Spanish also visited the region during this period; Angel de Villafane explored the area in 1561 and Hernando de Soto searched for gold in the southwestern portion of the state in 1540. None of these explorers attempted to establish permanent settlements.

In 1584, Queen Elizabeth of England gave Sir Walter Raleigh permission to explore and settle the region. He sent out a preliminary expedition to scout the area and select a location for a permanent colony. The explorers selected Roanoke Island and a group of 108 male settlers attempted to colonize the region in 1585. They were unable to cope with the many hardships and returned to England the following year. Although it ended in failure, this colony was notable for being the first attempt by English-speaking people to colonize America.

In 1587, another attempt was made to colonize Roanoke Island. This time the settlement group included women and children, as well as men. Virginia Dare was born on August 18, 1587, the first child of English-speaking parents to be born in America. Nine days after her birth, her grandfather John White, governor of the colony, returned to England to obtain more supplies for the colony. He was unable to return for three years, due to the war between England and Spain. When he returned to Roanoke in 1590, all the settlers had disappeared. He found the letters "CRO" carved into a tree on the beach and the word "Croatoan" carved on a post. There are a number of theories regarding the fate of the colonists but the mystery of this "Lost Colony" is still unsolved today.

North Carolina in the 17th Century

The next attempt to colonize this area took place in 1629, when King Charles I of England granted the area south of Albermarle Sound in Virginia to his Attorney General, Sir Robert Heath. The King named the area Carolana but Heath was unable to attempt the settlement of the region. In 1663, King Charles II changed the name of the area to Carolina and granted it to a group of eight lords known as the Lords Proprietors. They, and their descendants, controlled the area until 1729. The first permanent settlement in Carolina was Albermarle County, later followed by another in the area that would become Charleston, South Carolina. Between 1692 and 1712, North and South Carolina were united under one governmental authority, with the governor of Carolina located in Charleston and a deputy governor in North Carolina.

North Carolina in the 18th Century

In 1711, Carolina became involved in a war with the Tuscarora Indians over land and the settlers' treatment of the Indians. The Tuscarora attacked colonists near the town of New Bern on September 22 and killed over 130 settlers. The survivors fled to Bath and the governor appealed to South Carolina for assistance. In early 1712, South Carolina sent an army of soldiers and Yamasee Indians. The army won two decisive battles in 1712 and eventually ended the war in 1713.

During the early part of the 18th century, people moved to North Carolina from both South Carolina and Virginia. In addition, settlers from France, Germany, and Switzerland came to the region. Increased controversy over the exact boundary between Virginia and North Carolina led to an agreement in 1728. A group of commissioners that represented both colonies selected a point on the Atlantic coast and surveyed a line west. This line was accepted as the border between the two colonies.

In 1729, North Carolina became a royal colony when seven of the eight Lords Proprietors sold their interests in the region to King George II of Great Britain. The one Lord Proprietor who refused to sell, John Carteret, was given a tract of land near the Virginia border. This region became known as the Granville District. It was abolished during the American Revolution and the lands were confiscated by the new state. Colonial government did not change significantly because of this sale, except that colonial officials were appointed by the Lords Proprietors during the proprietary period and by the Crown during the later royal period. By some accounts, the royal governors were more capable than the proprietary governors. The colony developed a bicameral (two-house) legislature and new courts were created.

In 1767, New Bern, located in the eastern portion of the colony, was selected as the permanent capital. Western settlers were highly opposed to this because it placed all local governmental activities in the east and made it difficult for westerners to obtain access to colony government. In 1768, wealthy landowners in the western portion of the colony organized the Regulator Movement in a rebellion against unfair, corrupt, and oppressive governmental practices. There were a number of riots and other acts of violence. However, in 1771, Governor William Tryon ordered the colonial militia to fight a group of 2,000 Regulators at Alamance Creek. The Regulators were defeated. Over 6,000 Regulators were pardoned and many of them subsequently left North Carolina, although six were hanged for treason against the Crown.

In the 1760s and 1770s, North Carolina, along with other colonies, began to rebel against their enforced colonial status. Acts such as the Stamp Act of 1765 and the Townshend Act of 1767, which were enacted by the British Parliament without the consent of the colonists, led to anger and rebellion. Resistance was coordinated among the colonies. For example, when Massachusetts was punished by the Crown for resisting the 1773 Tea Act, North Carolina sent food supplies to the stricken colony. In 1774, the colony's first provincial congress selected delegates to be sent to the First Continental Congress in Philadelphia. North Carolina was a divided colony; while the popularly-elected legislature opposed the royal governor, Josiah Martin, many people, even those who opposed parliamentary taxation, were opposed to the idea of a war with England. By the middle of 1775, the colony was divided into two main groups: patriots who were willing to fight for independence and conservative loyalists who, while they had grievances with England, did not want to go to war over them.

The American Revolution began in Massachusetts in April, 1775, with the Battles of Lexington and Concord. Governor Martin fled the capital, first to Fort Johnston on the lower Cape Fear River, and then to a British warship. He developed plans to regain control of North Carolina, received approval from Britain, and began to raise an army of loyalists, or Tories as they were known. However, the Battle of Moore's Creek Bridge, which took place on February 27, 1776, resulted in the defeat of the loyalists by the patriots. The only other Revolutionary War battle to be fought in North Carolina occurred on March 15, 1781 at Guilford Courthouse. The battle, which lasted only three hours, is generally considered to be a strategic victory for the colonists, because the British troops were so weakened by the battle that General Charles Cornwallis was forced to withdraw out of the Carolinas and move north to Yorktown, Virginia. After Cornwallis' surrender in October, all British forces evacuated North Carolina and there was no further revolutionary activity in the colony.

On April 17, 1776 the fourth provincial congress met at Halifax and authorized the colony's delegation to the Continental Congress to vote for independence. The passage of the Halifax Resolves was the first official action of any colony calling for independence from Great Britain. The Declaration of Independence was signed by three representatives from the colony: John Penn, William Hooper, and Joseph Hewes.

The first state constitution was adopted in December 1776 by the fifth provincial congress. The first governor under the new constitution was Richard Caswell, who was elected on December 21, 1776. The constitution was drafted and adopted without submission to the people. An examination of the constitution shows the congress' fear of giving too much power to the executive branch. The state governor served a term of only one year and could serve only three terms in six years.

After the war, North Carolina participated in the Constitutional Convention of 1787, to develop the first United States Constitution. North Carolina was in favor of equal representation of all states in the Senate, despite its stature as the fourth largest state by population. One of the North Carolina delegates was also responsible for suggesting the six year senatorial term. In 1788, North Carolina refused to ratify the new United States constitution. However, on November 21, 1789, the state did adopt the constitution and became the 12th state to enter the union. That same year, the University of North Carolina was chartered, becoming the first public university in the country. In 1794, the state capital was moved to Raleigh.

North Carolina in the 19th Century

During the early part of the 19th century, North Carolina was nicknamed the "Rip Van Winkle" state because it made so little progress that many said it was asleep. North Carolina was primarily a one-party state, favoring the Democratic-Republican party which focused on states rights, and opposing a strong federal government. It was not until the 1830s that a second party, the Whigs, began to emerge in the state.

In 1835, a state constitutional convention was held in Raleigh and a number of new amendments were adopted. One resulted in a change in the method of electing the governor. Instead of being elected by the legislature and serving for one year, the governor was to be elected by the people (the adult male taxpayers of the state) and serve for a period of two years. Other changes included a change in the membership of the House and the Senate, fixing the Senate at 50 members and the House at 120, and the abolishment of the right of free blacks to vote.

Partly as a result of the changes to the state constitution, the state saw an increased interest in government, greater concern on the part of government for the welfare of the people, and the development of a two-party system. The Whig Party controlled the government from 1836 to 1850, primarily representing the non-slave areas in the western portion of the state. After 1850, the Democratic Party, which was mainly dominated by slaveowners in the eastern parts of the state, obtained control of the government. This was a period of significant advancement for the state. Roads and railroads were built and an excellent public school system was established. The tax system was reformed as was the criminal law, with some of the harsher penalties left over from the British common law system abolished. At the same time, however, North Carolina had one of the highest rates of illiteracy among the southern states and the legal rights of free blacks were increasingly restricted.

North Carolina, like most southern states, was fiercely protective of its rights to own slaves. The institution of slavery was seen by many southerners as an essential part of their economic system, which centered around cotton, and the Northern movement to abolish slavery was viewed as an attempt to dominate the economy of the United States. Originally, despite the number of slave owners in the state, North Carolina supported the Union. In 1860, South Carolina seceded and the Civil War began in April, 1861. North Carolina originally attempted to work for a compromise but on May 20, 1861, a state convention voted for secession after realizing that many North Carolina citizens would be unwilling to fight against fellow Southerners. Although most of the fighting of the Civil War occurred in other states, there were several significant battles that took place in North Carolina, including the battles of Fort Hatteras, Plymouth, New Bern, and Bentonville. North

Carolina supplied more soldiers and supplies to the Confederacy than any other state in the Confederate States of America. North Carolina also lost more soldiers, over 40,000, than any other Confederate state; approximately 25 percent of all Confederate casualties were from North Carolina.

In 1865, a state convention repealed the ordinance of secession and abolished slavery in North Carolina. However, the state also adopted the Black Codes, which restricted the former black slaves to second-class citizenship. In 1868, the state legislature ratified the new 14th Amendment to the U.S. Constitution, which made all former slaves U.S. citizens and allowed black men to vote for delegates to state constitutional conventions. After ratifying this Amendment, North Carolina was readmitted to the United States.

That same year, a new state constitution was adopted, significantly changing the government of the state. The new constitution required all major state officers to be elected by the people, rather than by the legislature. All executive officers, including the governor, were to serve four-year terms while supreme court justices and superior court judges were elected to eight-year terms. The people were given the power to elect all key state executive officers, judges, county officials, and legislators. The constitution also eliminated the previous property qualifications for both voting and holding office in the state, thus allowing all adult men in North Carolina to vote. The elections of 1868 were dominated by the newly formed Republican Party of North Carolina.

During the next few years, dissatisfaction with the Republican administration in the state increased, particularly among whites who disliked the participation of blacks in government. Taxes rose significantly, the state debt doubled, and corruption flourished. In 1872, the Democratic/Conservative Party, running on a platform of Republican abuses of power, regained control of the state legislature with the help of the Ku Klux Klan, who mounted a campaign of threats and violence to keep blacks and Republicans from going to the polls. A constitutional convention in 1875 resulted in the adoption of 30 new amendments, all of which were ratified by public vote. Included were a prohibition on secret political societies, the establishment of a State Department of Agriculture, a reduction in the membership of the state Supreme Court (decreasing it from five to three justices), and the establishment of a one-year residency requirement for voting in the state. One key amendment returned control of local government to the state legislature (i.e., the Democratic Party). The Democratic Party controlled the legislature and the government for the next 20 years, and focused on keeping whites in power.

During this period, textile and furniture industries grew rapidly in the state. The plantation system was replaced by sharecropping and tenant farming, which remained until World War II. Many sharecroppers and tenant farmers fell into debt in this system. In 1892, many of the farmers in the state joined together to form the People's Party as an expression of their dissatisfaction with the Democratic Party then in power. The People's Party, part of a political movement known as populism, was able to win some offices in the 1892 elections but was unable to become the majority party. During the 1894 elections, the populists and the Republicans cooperated, creating a "Fusion" ticket which was able to gain control of the legislature and, for a very brief period, the governorship of the state. The Fusionists focused on political equality, not only allowing blacks to vote freely but also allowing them to be elected to the state legislature.

In 1898, the Democrats regained control of the legislature and the governorship, using a race-based campaign. The voters in this election also approved a constitutional amendment that required a literacy test, as a way of removing blacks from participation in politics. Racial segregation began in the state, with state laws requiring separate public facilities for whites and blacks. These included drinking fountains, restrooms, schools, restaurants, and laundries.

North Carolina in the 20th Century

The populist movement basically disappeared in the early 20th century, due in part to the defeats in the elections of 1898 and 1900, as well as to the improved economic climate for farmers. The Democratic Party dominated and controlled the government of North Carolina continuously from 1901 until 1973. In addition, until 1973, every individual elected to the U.S. Senate from North Carolina was a Democrat.

In 1903, the first successful powered flight was made by Wilbur and Orville Wright at Kitty Hawk, North Carolina.

The state was hit hard by the Great Depression but was greatly assisted by the various federal public works programs and by federal programs designed to help farmers. Unemployment in the state decreased significantly during World War II as over 360,000 soldiers from North Carolina went into the armed services. In addition, the federal government spent almost $2 billion in North Carolina on contracts for war materials. A total of 83 industrial plants in the state supplied materials to defense agencies.

After the war, industry in North Carolina expanded. Many businesses moved to North Carolina because of the state's restrictions on labor unions. Cities expanded as people looking for jobs moved out of rural farming areas into urban environments. The labor movement did not gain effective bargaining power in the state until 1974, when the Amalgamated Clothing and Textile Workers Union culminated eleven years of organizing efforts and won the right to unionize at eight textile plants in the state.

In 1954, the U.S. Supreme Court decided in the case of *Brown v. Board of Education* that segregated schools were unconstitutional.[1] Although North Carolina was less resistant to the concept of desegregation than many other southern states, the legislature was opposed to desegregating the public schools. In 1955, three black applicants were admitted under federal court order to the University of North Carolina at Chapel Hill. In 1957, three school boards[2] began to integrate the public schools and this gradually spread throughout the state.

During the Civil Rights Movement of the 1960s, Greensboro, North Carolina was notable as the originator of the mass sit-in, which attempted to force segregated lunch counters to provide integrated service. Although integrated service (serving both blacks and whites together in the same restaurant) began to appear in many larger cities in North Carolina, many smaller towns continued the policy of segregated service until 1964, when it was outlawed by the passage of the federal Civil Rights Act.

In 1967, in response to a suggestion by then-Governor Dan Moore, the North Carolina State Bar and the North Carolina Bar Association joined forces to create the joint North Carolina State Constitution Study Commission. The purpose of the Commission was to study the need for revisions of the state constitution. The eventual result of the Commission's work resulted in the proposal of a new Constitution of 1971, which, after passing through the House and Senate, was ratified by the voters in the 1970 general election and took effect on July 1, 1971. Five constitutional amendments were also ratified at this election.

In 1972, the first Republican governor in North Carolina since 1901 and the first Republican U.S. Senator since 1895 were elected. This marked the end of the one-party rule that had characterized the state during the 20th century.

During the late 20th century, North Carolina's economic structure began to change. Tobacco and textiles, both major parts of the state's economy for over a century, began to falter. At the same time, the development of high-tech research and development industries increased in the 1990s, spurred on by the Research Triangle Park, which was created in 1959, and which is located between Durham, Chapel Hill, and Raleigh. As a result of programs such as the Research Triangle Park, the number of high-tech and professional jobs has increased significantly in the state. Currently, manufacturing remains the state's principle economic activity.

NORTH CAROLINA TODAY

North Carolina is the 29rd largest state in the country, with a total land area of 48,718 square miles, as well as 3,954 square miles of inland water. The average elevation of the state is approximately 700 feet above sea level. From east to west, the widest portion of the state measures 503 miles; the longest portion from north to south measures 187 miles.

Currently, North Carolina is the 11th most populous state in the country. The 2000 census[3] reported a total population of 8,049,313, an increase of 21.4 percent over the 1990 figure, making North Carolina one of the fastest-growing states in the country. The population density of the state was 165.2 persons per square mile. Approximately 25 percent of the population were under the age of 18 and 12 percent of the population were 65 years or older. The most populous city in the state is Charlotte, with a population of 540,828 in 2000. Other cities with a population of over 100,000 include Raleigh (the state capital), Greensboro, Durham, Winston-Salem, and Fayetteville. Mecklenberg County is the largest county by population, with 695,454 inhabitants in 2000.[4]

According to the 2000 census[5], approximately 72 percent of the state's population are white and 21.6 percent are black. Approximately 5 percent of the population are reported as being of Hispanic or Latino origin, although they may be of any race. Only 5.3 percent of North Carolina residents are foreign born, less than half the national figure of 11.1 percent.

North Carolina has a total of 100 counties. The state elects two United States Senators and 12 members of the House of Representatives, for a total of 14 electoral votes. The current state constitution was adopted in 1971.

NOTES

1.   *Brown v. Board of Education*, 347 U.S. 483 (1954)
2.   The first three school boards in North Carolina to integrate their public schools were Charlotte, Winston-Salem, and Greensboro.
3.   United States Census Bureau (http://www.census.gov)
4.   North Carolina State Data Center (http://census.state.nc.us/)
5.   United States Census Bureau, *op. cit.*

CHAPTER 2

INTRODUCTION TO NORTH CAROLINA CRIMINAL LAW

THE STRUCTURE OF THE GOVERNMENT

North Carolina criminal law is found in the state constitution and in the North Carolina General Statutes. Both have been frequently modified, amended, and altered over the past 150 years.

The first **North Carolina Constitution**[1] was adopted in 1776 by the Fifth Provincial Congress of North Carolina. The second was adopted in 1868 and the current (third) constitution was adopted in 1971. The North Carolina Constitution is the primary law of the state, although it is of course subordinate to the United States Constitution. No criminal law or constitutional amendment enacted in North Carolina may conflict with or violate any individual rights which are guaranteed by the U.S. Constitution, the Bill of Rights, any other Constitutional Amendments, or any federal laws. If any part of the North Carolina constitution or legal code is found to be in conflict with the U.S. Constitution or federal statutes, the North Carolina enactment is unconstitutional and must be changed.

There are several ways in which the constitution may be amended or revised. These are described in Article XIII of the North Carolina Constitution, which states that:

> The people of this State reserve the power to amend this Constitution and to adopt
> a new or revised Constitution. This power may be exercised by either of the
> methods set out hereinafter in this Article, but in no other way.[2]

First, a constitutional convention, known as a **Convention of the People of North Carolina**, may be called for the purpose of proposing a new Constitution, revisions to the current Constitution, or amendments to the current Constitution. If the Convention adopts a proposal, it must be submitted to the voters of the state for ratification.[3] For such a Convention to be called, there must be an agreement by two-thirds of the members of each house of the **North Carolina General Assembly** as well as a majority vote in favor of the Convention by the qualified voters of the state.[4]

Second, a new Constitution, Constitutional revision, or new amendments to the current Constitution may be proposed by a joint resolution that is agreed to by three-fifths of the membership of each house of the North Carolina General Assembly. This proposal must also be presented to the voters for ratification.[5]

In all cases, any proposals that are approved by the voters at a general election will become effective on the next January first after ratification unless a different effective date is prescribed by the Convention or in the act presented to the voters by the Assembly.

Like most states, North Carolina has three branches of government: executive, legislative, and judicial.

The Executive Branch

Article III of the North Carolina Constitution discusses North Carolina's **Executive Branch**, which consists of a governor, a lieutenant governor, and nineteen executive departments. Eight of these department heads, as well as the governor and lieutenant governor, are elected to four-year terms. These departments include the Secretary of State, the Office of the State Auditor, the State Treasurer, and the Departments of Agriculture, Insurance, Justice, Labor, and Public Instruction.[6] These elected officials form the **Council of State**. The remaining department heads are known as "secretaries" and are appointed by the governor. The departments with appointed department heads include the North Carolina Community College System and the Departments of Administration, Commerce, Correction, Crime Control and Public Safety, Cultural Resources, Health and Human Services, Juvenile Justice and Delinquency Prevention, Revenue, Transportation, and Environment and Natural Resources.

The governor and lieutenant governor serve four-year terms and are limited to two consecutive terms, although they may serve any number of years. To be elected to the offices of governor or lieutenant governor of North Carolina, candidates must, at the time of election, be at least 30 years of age, a U.S. citizen for at least five years, and a resident of North Carolina for the preceding two years.[7] Qualifications for the other elected posts are similar, except that only an individual who is authorized to practice law in the state may be eligible to become Attorney General.[8]

The duties of the governor are specifically listed in the Constitution.[9] They include:

(1)   Residence. The Governor shall reside at the seat of government of this State.

(2)   Information to General Assembly. The Governor shall from time to time give the General Assembly information of the affairs of the State and recommend to their consideration such measures as he shall deem expedient.

(3)   Budget. The Governor shall prepare and recommend to the General Assembly a comprehensive budget of the anticipated revenue and proposed expenditures of the State for the ensuing fiscal period. The budget as enacted by the General Assembly shall be administered by the Governor...

(4)   Execution of laws. The Governor shall take care that the laws be faithfully executed.

(5)   Commander in Chief. The Governor shall be Commander in Chief of the military forces of the State except when they shall be called into the service of the United States.

(6)   Clemency. The Governor may grant reprieves, commutations, and pardons, after conviction, for all offenses (except in cases of impeachment), upon such conditions as he may think proper, subject to regulations prescribed by law

relative to the manner of applying for pardons. The terms reprieves, commutations, and pardons shall not include paroles.

(7) Extra sessions. The Governor may, on extraordinary occasions, by and with the advice of the Council of State, convene the General Assembly in extra session by his proclamation, stating therein the purpose or purposes for which they are thus convened.

(8) Appointments. The Governor shall nominate and by and with the advice and consent of a majority of the Senators appoint all officers whose appointments are not otherwise provided for.

(9) Information. The Governor may at any time require information in writing from the head of any administrative department or agency upon any subject relating to the duties of his office.

(10) Administrative reorganization. The General Assembly shall prescribe the functions, powers, and duties of the administrative departments and agencies of the State and may alter them from time to time, but the Governor may make such changes in the allocation of offices and agencies and in the allocation of those functions, powers, and duties as he considers necessary for efficient administration. If those changes affect existing law, they shall be set forth in executive orders, which shall be submitted to the General Assembly not later than the sixtieth calendar day of its session, and shall become effective and shall have the force of law upon adjournment sine die of the session, unless specifically disapproved by resolution of either house of the General Assembly or specifically modified by joint resolution of both houses of the General Assembly.

(11) Reconvened sessions. The Governor shall, when required by Section 22 of Article II of this Constitution, reconvene a session of the General Assembly. At such reconvened session, the General Assembly may only consider such bills as were returned by the Governor to that reconvened session for reconsideration...

On January 1, 2001, Michael F. Easley took office as governor of North Carolina. His present term expires in 2005 and he may be re-elected to one successive term.

The Legislative Branch

The **General Assembly** of North Carolina, which is discussed in Article II of the North Carolina Constitution, is the lawmaking branch of the state government. The Assembly is made up of two houses: a 50-member Senate and a 120-member House of Representatives. The Assembly meets annually and all members, regardless of house, are elected to two-year terms. This is unusual; in many states (and in the federal government) the length of the term served by senators is longer than the term served by members of the House of Representatives. Meetings are held annually in Raleigh.

Each member of the Assembly represents one senatorial or house district. There is no limit to the number of times members of the legislature may be re-elected. Qualifications differ for Senators and Representatives. To serve as a member of the North Carolina Senate, candidates must be at least 25 years of age, a qualified voter of the state, have been resident in North Carolina as a citizen for at least two years prior to the election, and have been resident in the district for which elected for at least one year prior to the election.[10] To serve as a member of the North Carolina House of Representatives, candidates must be a qualified voter of the state and have been resident in the district for which elected for at least one year prior to the election.[11] Members take office on the first day of January immediately following election.[12]

The lieutenant governor of North Carolina serves as President of the Senate, although s/he has no vote in the Senate except as a tie-breaker.[13] All other Assembly officers, including the Speaker of the House of Representatives, are elected by the members.

The Assembly can enact five different types of statutes or laws. First, it may create laws that regulate the conduct of individuals, either prohibiting or requiring certain actions. If the law includes a punishment for violation, such as a fine or imprisonment, it is a criminal law. Second, the Assembly may enact laws that deal with services the state provides, such as schools, public recreation facilities, and health services. Third, the Assembly may create laws that allow or require local governmental units to act in some manner. Fourth, the Assembly may enact laws relating to taxes and appropriations, and that determine how much money the state shall raise and how it shall spend this money. Finally, the Assembly has the power to propose amendments to the North Carolina Constitution.

The Judicial Branch

The judicial branch of the government, which is discussed in Article IV of the North Carolina Constitution, contains the various North Carolina courts. These are divided into three divisions. The **Appellate Division** includes the **North Carolina Supreme Court** and the **Court of Appeals**.[14] The Supreme Court is made up of seven justices, one of whom is appointed the Chief Justice.[15] The number of justices serving on the Court of Appeals is determined by the Assembly, but it may not be less than five members.[16] The **Superior Court** and **District Court Divisions** are trial courts. Judges in the appellate and superior court divisions serve eight-year terms while district court judges serve terms of four years. The North Carolina court system is discussed in more detail in Chapter 5.

Passing a Law in North Carolina

In North Carolina, a bill, or proposed law, must be introduced into either the Senate or the House of Representatives by a member of the General Assembly, who is known as the sponsor of the bill. The bill is then assigned to a committee who studies it and makes a recommendation regarding approval. The committee, or any member of the Assembly, may also recommend or propose amendments to the bill. After the bill is approved by the committee, it is placed before the full membership of the legislative house into which it was introduced for discussion and debate. After the bill is passed by one legislative house, it must go through the same procedure in the other house (committee review, committee approval, debate, vote). If amendments are made, both houses must agree to the changes.

After a bill passes both houses of the General Assembly, it is **enrolled**. This means that a clean copy, containing any amendments, is prepared for the signatures of the two presiding officers of the General Assembly. After these signatures are obtained, the bill is **ratified**.

In 1996, North Carolina voters approved an amendment to the North Carolina Constitution which allows for a gubernatorial veto of public bills[17]. The day after a bill is ratified, it is presented to the governor for approval or veto. If the governor approves and signs the bill, or if he fails to veto it within ten days, the bill will become law. The Assembly may, by a three-fifths vote of each house, enact a bill into law over the governor's veto.

THE NORTH CAROLINA STATE CRIMINAL LAW

There are several sources of criminal law in North Carolina. These include:

- federal and state constitutions
- statutory criminal law
- common law
- case law

Together, the North Carolina Constitution and the U.S. Constitution provide the basic framework for criminal law, first by focusing on individual rights and on the limitations placed on government power and second, by requiring the establishment of a judicial system. However, neither the federal nor the state constitution significantly emphasizes the creation or definition of crimes.

The primary source of **statutory criminal law** in North Carolina is the North Carolina Criminal Law, which is codified in Chapter 14 of the North Carolina General Statutes (NCGS).[18] However, other statutes also contain laws which relate to crime and punishment. For example, Chapter 7B of the General Statutes, the Juvenile Code, contains law relating to crimes committed by juveniles. Other chapters deal with topics such as evidence[19], jury selection[20], and criminal procedure[21].

The North Carolina General Statutes was originally based on the English **common law**, which became the law of the original thirteen colonies and then evolved into the law of the individual states as they entered the union. The common law developed out of common customs and usages that developed over a very long period of time. Statutory law is based on these common law principles. NCGS §4-1 states that:

> All such parts of the common law as were heretofore in force and use within this State, or so much of the common law as is not destructive of, or repugnant to, or inconsistent with, the freedom and independence of this State and the form of government therein established, and which has not been otherwise provided for in whole or in part, not abrogated, repealed, or become obsolete, are hereby declared to be in full force within this State.

Because of this, state courts may use the common law to analyze and interpret the state's criminal code. If a specific crime is not defined in the statutes, the common law definition would be applicable. However, if a statute supercedes the common law, that statute becomes the controlling law for that issue.

Unlike some states, many criminal law issues in North Carolina are not found in the statutory law. For example, in many states, a statute will specifically define a crime and list all the elements that must exist for a suspect to be charged with the offense. However, in North Carolina, the statutes frequently do not include a listing of the elements of a crime. This means that the definition of the illegal act is found in the common law. For example, the General Statutes only specifically define the crime of armed robbery.[22] Any other type of robbery (e.g., one committed without a firearm or other dangerous weapon) is classified as a Class G felony.[23] However, the statutes do not include a definition of the crime of robbery. It is necessary to turn to the common law to obtain an understanding of the elements required to convict a defendant of the crime of robbery.[24]

Case law consists of appellate court decisions or opinions which interpret the meaning of the statutory and common law. Effectively, case law is made by judges when they hand down decisions in court. Because of the principle of *stare decisis*, or precedent, a decision made by a judge in one court will be followed by later judges in the state until the same court reverses its decision or until the decision is overturned by a higher court.

The North Carolina General Statutes contains two types of statutory criminal law: substantive and procedural. **Substantive criminal law** includes definitions of specific crimes and identifies the punishments associated with each criminal act. NCGS §14-17, the section of the General Statutes that defines murder in the first and second degree, is an example of substantive criminal law. **Procedural law**, on the other hand, focuses on the methods that are used to enforce substantive criminal law. In other words, procedural law outlines the rules that the state must follow when dealing with crimes and criminals. These include the procedures that must be used to investigate crimes, arrest suspects, and carry out formal prosecution. The section of the General Statutes which discusses a consent search and seizure is an example of procedural law.[25]

THE DEFINITION AND CLASSIFICATION OF CRIME

There are two types of crimes in North Carolina, **felonies** and **misdemeanors**. These are defined in NCGS §14-1, which states that:

> A felony is a crime which:
> (1) Was a felony at common law;
> (2) Is or may be punishable by death;
> (3) Is or may be punishable by imprisonment in the State's prison; or
> (4) Is denominated as a felony by statute.
> Any other crime is a misdemeanor.

It is clear from this definition that, in many cases, the difference between a felony and a misdemeanor is not determined by the action committed by the offender but by the possible punishment prescribed in the General Statutes. Even if the criminal or common law does not specifically identify a crime as a misdemeanor or a felony, the classification can easily be inferred from the prescribed sentence.

In addition, the state recognizes a category of noncriminal violations known as **infractions**. These are defined in NCGS §14-3.1(a), which states that:

> An infraction is a noncriminal violation of law not punishable by imprisonment. Unless otherwise provided by law, the sanction for a person found responsible for an infraction is a penalty of not more than one hundred dollars ($100.00). The proceeds of penalties for infractions are payable to the county in which the infraction occurred for the use of the public schools.

North Carolina divides felonies into categories, based on the seriousness of the offense. The most serious category is a Class A felony. Felonies are punishable by death or by imprisonment in a state prison for a period of at least one year. In addition to these punishments, the offender may also be fined. The classification of a felony is generally listed in the statute defining the offense. Sentences are based on the structured sentencing guidelines found in Chapter 15A, Article 81B of the General Statutes. Structured sentencing in North Carolina will be discussed in more detail in Chapter 6.

Misdemeanors are classified into Class 1, 2, and 3. Punishments for most misdemeanors are listed in the statute defining the offense. According to NCGS §14-3, in most cases, a misdemeanor with a maximum punishment of a fine only, or imprisonment for 30 days or less, is considered to be a Class 3 misdemeanor. A misdemeanor with a punishment of 31 days to six months imprisonment is considered to be Class 2, and a misdemeanor with a maximum punishment of more than six months imprisonment is a Class 1 misdemeanor.

The Criminal Act (*Actus Reus*) and Intent (*Mens Rea*)

In North Carolina, for an individual to be considered criminally liable for his or her behavior, two key elements are necessary: ***actus reus*** (a criminal act) and ***mens rea*** (a guilty mind).

The first element, *actus reus*, involves a voluntary act committed by the offender. Most criminal acts are deliberate and voluntary. However, the act necessary to make up a crime will vary with each crime. Verbal actions (words) can be a sufficient action in, for example, the crime of perjury. Merely possessing something may be a sufficient act if the crime is one that involves illegal possession of goods (for example, possession of illegal drugs).

In some cases, a criminal act may also consist of an omission or failure to act. An **omission** occurs when someone who has a legal duty to act fails to perform an action that is required by law. For example, a security guard who deliberately looks the other way while company property is stolen is a passive participant and is guilty of an omission. Similarly, a parent or other legal caretaker who fails to adequately feed and shelter an infant, resulting in the death of the child, has committed a crime by his or her failure to act.

Failing to act is only a crime of omission when an individual has a legal duty to act in that situation. For example, consider the case of a swimmer at a local public pool who develops a cramp while in deep water. The lifeguard who is on duty at the pool has a legal duty to act and, if he/she fails to go to the swimmer's assistance, would be guilty of a crime of omission. However, the other swimmers in the pool have only a moral duty to aid the distressed swimmer and if they fail to provide assistance would not be guilty of any crime. In addition, the omission or failure to act must also be voluntary.

Mens rea involves the offender's mental state at the time of the criminal action. In addition to the voluntary criminal act, a **culpable mental state** may also be required. A culpable mental state means that the crime is committed intentionally, knowingly, recklessly, or with criminal negligence. A crime is committed **intentionally** when the offender consciously desires the outcome. Because intent is basically a state of mind, the offender does not have to declare intent to be convicted of a crime; intent may be inferred by the actions of the offender. A crime is committed **knowingly** when the offender is aware that his or her conduct violates the law. However, the offender does not need to be aware that his or her conduct will cause a certain outcome defined by an offense. A crime is committed **recklessly** when the offender is aware of the risk created by his/her actions and consciously and unjustifiably disregards that risk. It may not always be necessary to prove the offender is personally aware of the risk, only that a reasonable person would consider the behavior as creating grave risk. Finally, **criminal negligence** occurs when the offender fails to recognize a risk that would be perceived by any reasonable person.

Strict liability offenses are crimes for which a culpable mental state, or *mens rea*, is not required. In these situations, the act alone, regardless of the offender's state of mind at the time of the act, is enough to create criminal liability. Strict liability crimes are fairly rare. One example of a strict liability crime is statutory rape, which involves intercourse with a person who is between the ages of 13 and 15. A mistaken belief that the participant was not a minor is not a defense against such crimes in North Carolina.

DEFENSES TO A CRIMINAL CHARGE

There are a wide variety of defenses to a criminal charge. Many of these are specifically mentioned in the North Carolina General Statutes.

Justifications

A defendant who uses a **justification** defense admits to the commission of the criminal act but also claims that it was necessary to commit the act in order to avoid some greater evil or harm. Essentially, the defendant is not guilty of the crime s/he has been charged with because the reason for committing the act is one that the law considers to be a valid justification.

Probably the most well-known justification defense is that of **self-defense**, in which the defendant claims that the use of force against the victim was justifiable because it was the only way the defendant could ensure his/her own safety. Several statutes discuss the use of this defense as a defense for specific criminal acts. For example, NCGS §14-51.1 discusses the use of deadly force against a burglary. Essentially, the statute states that an individual in his/her place of residence may use any reasonable degree of force, including deadly force, against an intruder to prevent or terminate an unlawful entry by that intruder. There are several limitations on this. For example, the occupant must reasonably believe that the intruder may inflict serious bodily injury or death upon someone in the residence or the occupant must reasonably believe that the intruder intends to commit a felony in the residence.

Another justification defense is that of **consent**. This defense claims that the victim voluntarily consented to the actions that caused the injury and is most commonly used in sex-related offenses, such as sexual battery. For example, NCGS §14-27.7, which discusses intercourse and sexual offenses with certain victims (generally minors over whom the defendant has custodial responsibility), specifically states that consent is not a defense to any charge made under that section of the General Statutes.

Excuses

A defendant using an **excuse** defense is claiming that at the time of the criminal act some circumstance or personal condition creates a situation under which s/he should not be held criminally accountable. The defendant is essentially claiming that s/he is not responsible, and should not be blamed, for the act.

Probably the most well-known (and controversial) defense in this category is that of **insanity**. Although the term insanity is no longer used by mental health professionals, it is a legal term referring to a defense that is based on the defendant's claim that s/he was mentally ill or mentally incapacitated at the time of the offense. In North Carolina, to be found not guilty of a crime based on the insanity defense, a defendant must establish two facts:

1. The defendant must show that when the offense was committed, s/he had a mental disease or defect, or low intelligence

2. The defendant must show that as a result of this mental disease or defect, or low intelligence, s/he was incapable of understanding the nature of the act or of knowing that the act was wrong.[26]

Defendants who intend to present a defense of insanity must provide advance notice to the prosecution. NCGS §15A-959 mandates pretrial notification of intent to rely on the insanity defense within a specified period of time. If the defendant plans to introduce any expert testimony to support his/her claim, pretrial notification of this must also be filed with the court. If the defense files these motions, and the state consents, the court may conduct a pretrial hearing on the issue of the defendant's insanity. All defendants are presumed sane so the burden of proof is on the defense to prove the defendant was insane at the time of the crime. If the court finds that the defendant has a valid defense of insanity, s/he is found not guilty by reason of insanity (NGRI) and the judge will commit the defendant to a state 24-hour facility.[27] These are facilities designated for the custody and treatment of involuntary clients.[28] If the motion for a defense of insanity is denied, the hearing may not be referred to or brought into evidence at trial.

Another defense that falls into the category of excuses is that of **intoxication**. In most cases, voluntary intoxication is not a defense to any crime proscribed by law. However, if the crime with which the defendant is charged is a specific intent crime, the level of intoxication may suffice to negate that element of the crime if the intoxication was sufficient to prevent the defendant from forming the necessary intent. This does not preclude the defendant from being convicted of a lesser included offense. For example, while the level of intoxication may negate the specific intent necessary to sustain a charge of first degree murder (which requires premeditation and deliberation), it does not necessarily prevent a conviction of second degree murder (which requires malice, not specific intent). Voluntary intoxication is not a defense for any crime that does not require specific intent.

According to NCGS §14-455(a), "It is a defense to a charge of being intoxicated and disruptive in a public place that the defendant suffers from alcoholism." If a defendant is found not guilty to the charge of being intoxicated and disruptive in a public placed because s/he suffers from alcoholism, the court has the right to retain jurisdiction over the defendant for up to 15 days to determine whether the defendant is a substance abuser and whether s/he is a danger to himself/herself or to others.

The defense of **duress** or **necessity** generally requires that the defendant have committed the crime of which s/he is accused because the defendant has a reasonable fear that s/he or another person faces imminent death or serious bodily injury if s/he does not commit the act. One example would be a defendant who breaks and enters a home because s/he observes someone in the home requires immediate medical attention. The defense of duress may also involve the claim that the defendant's actions were committed under the control or influence of another person. An example of this type of duress would be a defendant who committed a robbery because his or her child was being held hostage and threatened.

Basically, duress negates the intent required for the crime. Duress may not be used as a defense to a charge of homicide. However, NCGS §15A-2000(f)(5) specifically mentions duress as a mitigating circumstance that may be considered by the court when deciding between a sentence of death and one of life imprisonment.

Procedural Defenses

A **procedural defense** claims that some form of official procedure was not followed or that procedural law was not properly followed during the investigation or the prosecution of the crime. One procedural defense is the **denial of a speedy trial**. The right to a speedy trial is guaranteed by the Sixth Amendment to the United States Constitution. NCGS §15A-954(a) states that:

> The court on motion of the defendant must dismiss the charges stated in a criminal pleading if it determines that ... (3) The defendant has been denied a speedy trial as required by the Constitution of the United States and the Constitution of North Carolina.

Another issue is that of **double jeopardy**, which is discussed in the Fifth Amendment to the U.S. Constitution. NCGS §15A-954(a) states that

The court on motion of the defendant must dismiss the charges stated in a criminal pleading if it determines that ... (5) The defendant has previously been placed in jeopardy of the same offense.

However, double jeopardy does not apply to probable cause hearings. A probable cause hearing is held to determine whether there is probable cause to believe that the offense named in the charges was actually committed and whether there is probable cause to believe that the accused committed the offense. If the judge at a probable cause hearing finds no probable cause, the charges will be dismissed. However, NCGS §15A-612(b) specifically states that "No finding made by a judge under this section precludes the State from instituting a subsequent prosecution for the same offense." Thus, it is legally permissible for the charges to be dismissed at a probable cause hearing and for the defendant to be brought up on the same charges at a later date.

NOTES

1. The North Carolina Constitution may be viewed online by going to the homepage of the North Carolina General Assembly (http://www.ncleg.net/homePage.pl) and selecting the link for "NC Constitution."
2. North Carolina Constitution, Article XIII, §2
3. North Carolina Constitution, Article XIII, §3
4. North Carolina Constitution, Article XIII, §1
5. North Carolina Constitution, Article XIII, §4
6. North Carolina Constitution, Article III, §7
7. North Carolina Constitution, Article III, §2
8. North Carolina Constitution, Article III, §7(7)
9. North Carolina Constitution, Article III, §5
10. North Carolina Constitution, Article II, §6
11. North Carolina Constitution, Article II, §7
12. North Carolina Constitution, Article II, §9
13. North Carolina Constitution, Article II, §13
14. North Carolina Constitution, Article IV, §5
15. North Carolina Constitution, Article IV, §6
16. North Carolina Constitution, Article IV, §7
17. North Carolina Constitution, Article II, §22
18. The North Carolina General Statutes may be viewed online by going to the homepage of the North Carolina General Assembly (http://www.ncleg.net/homePage.pl) and selecting the link for "NC Statutes."
19. North Carolina General Statutes, Chapter 8
20. North Carolina General Statutes, Chapter 9
21. North Carolina General Statutes, Chapters 15 and 15A
22. North Carolina General Statutes, §14-87
23. North Carolina General Statutes, §14-87.1
24. Thornburg, T.H. (2000). *An Introduction to Law for North Carolinians*, 2nd ed. Chapel Hill, N.C.: University of North Carolina at Chapel Hill Institute of Government.
25. North Carolina General Statutes, Chapter 15A, Article 9

26. Farb, Robert L., ed. (2001). *North Carolina Crimes: A Guidebook on the Elements of Crime.* Chapel Hill, N.C.: University of North Carolina at Chapel Hill Institute of Government.
27. North Carolina General Statutes, §15A-1321(a)
28. North Carolina General Statutes, §122C-252

CHAPTER 3

INDEX CRIMES

INTRODUCTION

The Federal Bureau of Investigation annually publishes the ***Uniform Crime Reports***[1] (UCR), the most widely used source of official data on crime and criminals in the United States. Much of the UCR deals with **index crimes**, a set of eight serious offenses that the FBI uses as a measure of crime in the United States. They are also known as **Part I Offenses** and include four violent crimes and four property crimes. The eight index crimes measured by the FBI are:

- homicide
- forcible rape
- robbery
- aggravated assault
- burglary
- larceny-theft
- motor-vehicle theft
- arson

However, the definitions used by the FBI in compiling the UCR are not always the same as those found in the North Carolina General Statutes. This chapter will discuss in detail the definitions of these eight serious crimes as provided by the General Statutes.

CRIMINAL HOMICIDE

Homicide is the killing of one human being by another. If that killing is illegal, then it is a form of **criminal homicide**. The UCR includes the crimes of murder and nonnegligent manslaughter, which are defined as "the wilful (nonnegligent) killing of one human being by another."[2] In North Carolina, criminal homicide is discussed in Chapter 14, Article 6 of the General Statutes and includes the crimes of:

- murder in the first degree
- murder in the second degree
- manslaughter

First Degree Murder

First degree murder is defined in NCGS §14-17, which states that:

> A murder which shall be perpetrated by means of a nuclear, biological, or chemical weapon of mass destruction..., poison, lying in wait, imprisonment, starving, torture, or by any other kind of willful, deliberate, and premeditated killing, or which shall be committed in the perpetration or attempted perpetration of any arson, rape or a sex offense, robbery, kidnapping, burglary, or other felony committed or attempted with the use of a deadly weapon shall be deemed to be murder in the first degree...

This statute identifies two specific categories of first degree murder: **premeditated murder** and **felony murder**. The first category involves the premeditated killing of another person, which basically refers to a killing in which the intent to kill was formed before the killing itself actually took place. Felony murder, on the other hand, does not require that the offender had any premeditated intent to kill. It merely requires that the offender was engaged in one of a specified list of crimes and that death occurred as a consequence of and while the offender was committing or attempting to commit that crime. Intent only has to be proved for the underlying felony, not for the killing. Thus, even if a participant in the felony had no weapon, did not intend to hurt anyone, and did no actual physical harm, s/he can be held culpable if someone died during the commission of the felony. If the death occurred while the offender was engaged in the commission of a crime that is not specifically listed in the statute, then the offender is not guilty of first degree felony murder in the first degree, although the offender may still be guilty of a lower degree of murder. North Carolina's felony murder rule is based on the English common law.

Murder in the first degree is a Class A felony in North Carolina. According to NCGS §14-17,

> any person who commits such murder shall be punished with death or imprisonment in the State's prison for life without parole..., except that any such person who was under 17 years of age at the time of the murder shall be punished with imprisonment in the State's prison for life without parole.

North Carolina does not allow the death penalty to be imposed on an offender under the age of 17. The mandatory sentence for such an offender is life imprisonment without parole. The statute does include one exception to this provision: a person under the age of 17 who commits a first degree murder while already serving or while on escape from a sentence of imprisonment for a prior murder may be eligible for a sentence of death.

NCGS §15A-2000 discusses the proceedings involved in determining the sentence in a case of murder in the first degree. The process involves two separate phases. The first phase involves the determination of guilt in the crime of first degree murder. Then, if the State has given notice that it intends to seek the death penalty, the court holds a separate sentencing proceeding to determine whether the sentence will be death or imprisonment for life without parole.

Capital punishment in North Carolina is discussed in more detail in Chapter 7.

Second Degree Murder

Second degree murder is also discussed in NCGS §14-17. The statute states that:

> All other kinds of murder, including that which shall be proximately caused by the unlawful distribution of opium or any synthetic or natural salt, compound, derivative, or preparation of opium, or cocaine or other substance described in G.S. 90-90(1) d., when the ingestion of such substance causes the death of the user, shall be deemed murder in the second degree, and any person who commits such murder shall be punished as a Class B2 felon.

Essentially, second degree murder is any murder that does not fall under the definition of first degree murder in North Carolina. It generally involves an unplanned killing that results from a malicious act of some kind, when the defendant is reasonably aware that his/her actions may cause the death of another person. Malice occurs when one of the following three conditions is present:

1. The killing was committed with hatred, ill will, or resentment against the victim

2. The killing was caused by an act that is inherently dangerous to human life and that was committed recklessly and without regard to life

3. The killing was committed intentionally and without any excuse or justification.[3]

Specific intent to kill the victim is not required, only a general intent to commit an inherently dangerous act (including the unlawful distribution of a variety of illegal substances). Therefore, voluntary intoxication cannot be used as a defense against this crime. There is no crime in North Carolina of attempted second degree murder. This is because specific intent is not a required element of the crime of second degree murder and an attempt requires intent to commit the underlying offense.

Manslaughter

North Carolina recognizes two types of **manslaughter**.[4] **Voluntary manslaughter** involves the killing of another person without malice. The absence of malice is what distinguishes this crime from second degree murder. Essentially, voluntary manslaughter involves killing in the heat of passion or in an excessive attempt at self defense. This crime is a Class D felony.

Involuntary manslaughter is a Class F felony. It involves an unlawful death that occurs without malice, premeditation, deliberation, or an intent to kill or inflict serious bodily harm on the victim. Generally, this category of manslaughter is used for four types of deaths. The first includes those cases not covered by the felony murder rule. In other words, involuntary manslaughter may be used in the case of a death that occurred during the commission of a crime that was not listed in

NCGS §14-17. One of the most common examples of this type is a death due to reckless driving, such as a DWI offense. Another example would be a death resulting because a dog owner allowed his or her dogs to run free, when this act was a criminally negligent violation of a local ordinance. The second includes cases in which the death occurred as the result of an unlawful act that is not dangerous to life. An example of this type would be a death resulting from a minor assault because the victim was in some way especially vulnerable. The third category includes deaths resulting from a lawful act that was committed recklessly. Finally, the fourth category includes deaths that result from the offender's negligent failure to prevent harm to the victim. However, for an offender to be charged with this crime, the offender must have a legal duty to protect the victim.[5]

Non-Criminal Homicide

Although the UCR focuses specifically on criminal homicide, or murder, there are situations when the killing of one human being by another is lawful and therefore not a crime. Non-criminal homicides may be justifiable or excusable. An **excusable homicide** is a death that is caused by an accident or misfortune, when there is no unlawful intent involved in the act that caused the death. An automobile accident that does not involve negligence or any violation of the law on the part of the driver is an example of excusable homicide. A **justifiable homicide** is a killing that was committed by the use of justifiable deadly force, such as in self defense.

There are no punishments associated with justifiable or excusable homicides as they are not forms of criminal homicide. If a homicide is ruled justifiable or excusable, the defendant at trial must be acquitted and released.

FORCIBLE RAPE AND SEXUAL OFFENSES

In the Uniform Crime Reporting Program, **forcible rape** is defined as "the carnal knowledge of a female forcibly and against her will."[6] North Carolina recognizes two levels of forcible rape, first degree and second degree. In addition, the state recognizes the crimes of statutory rape and first and second degree sexual offenses.

First degree rape is defined in NCGS §14-27.2(a), which states that:

> A person is guilty of rape in the first degree if the person engages in vaginal intercourse:
> (1) With a victim who is a child under the age of 13 years and the defendant is at least 12 years old and is at least four years older than the victim; or
> (2) With another person by force and against the will of the other person, and:
>   a. Employs or displays a dangerous or deadly weapon or an article which the other person reasonably believes to be a dangerous or deadly weapon; or

     b. Inflicts serious personal injury upon the victim or another person; or

     c. The person commits the offense aided and abetted by one or more other persons.

First degree rape is a Class B1 felony in North Carolina.

Unlike the UCR definition, the North Carolina rape statute does not specify the gender of the victim. However, the requirement of vaginal intercourse does indicate that one of the participants must be female. The courts consider vaginal intercourse to be penile penetration of the vagina, vulva, or labia.[7] Therefore, in North Carolina, the defendant can be either male or female. For example, a woman who forces a man to have sexual intercourse with her could be found guilty of first degree forcible rape. However, the requirement of vaginal intercourse means that oral or anal intercourse, even if they are committed forcibly and without the victim's consent, are not considered to be first degree rape in North Carolina.

In addition to vaginal intercourse, one of two other conditions must be met for the defendant to be convicted of first degree rape. One is that the victim is under the age of 13 and the defendant is at least 12 years of age and at least four years older than the victim. The other condition requires that the intercourse be committed by force and against the will of the victim. This condition may involve one of three factors. First, the defendant may have used or displayed a dangerous or deadly weapon. Threatening with a weapon is sufficient to meet this condition; it is not necessary for the offender to actually use the weapon. Second, the defendant inflicted serious personal injury to the victim or another person. This may consist of physical injury, death, or mental injury, although for mental injury to qualify under this condition it must last for some time after the crime and must be greater than that normally experienced in every forcible rape. A victim who, for example, was so frightened by the rape that she was unable to return to her home for many months after the event, would satisfy this element. Third, the defendant was aided by others in the commission of the offense. The individual aiding and abetting the rape does not actually have to have sexual intercourse with the victim for this condition to be met.

Either condition is sufficient to sustain a charge of first degree rape. Thus, non-forcible vaginal intercourse with a child may be considered first degree rape under the first condition. Similarly, forcible vaginal intercourse with an individual over the age of 13 could also meet the statutory definition. Gang rape would also meet the criteria listed in the statute.

Second degree rape is a Class C felony. It is defined in NCGS §14-27.3(a), which states that:

> A person is guilty of rape in the second degree if the person engages in vaginal intercourse with another person:
> (1) By force and against the will of the other person; or
> (2) Who is mentally disabled, mentally incapacitated, or physically helpless, and the person performing the act knows or should

reasonably know the other person is mentally disabled, mentally incapacitated, or physically helpless.

Second degree rape is considered to be less serious than first degree rape. It also involves vaginal intercourse, requiring that one of the participants, either the perpetrator or the victim, must be female. Like the more serious crime, one of two other conditions in addition to vaginal intercourse must be met for a defendant to be convicted of second degree rape. The first is that the intercourse be committed by force and against the will of the victim. However, the statute does not require the presence of a weapon, the infliction of serious injury, or the assistance of others. Simple bodily force is sufficient to sustain the charge. The second condition is that the victim is mentally disabled or incapacitated or physically helpless and the defendant should reasonably have known this. These conditions are defined in NCGS 14-27.1. Mentally disabled essentially means the victim is mentally retarded or has a mental disorder that prevents the victim from understanding, resisting, or communicating unwillingness to submit to the sexual act. Mentally incapacitated means that some act has been committed upon the victim leaving him or her unable to understand or resist the sexual act. Physically helpless includes those victims who are unconscious and those who are physically unable to resist or communicate unwillingness to submit to the sexual act. A sleeping victim or one who is extremely intoxicated would be considered physically helpless. If the victim meets these conditions, the crime does not have to be committed by force for the act to be considered second degree rape.

In addition to rape, North Carolina also recognizes other crimes involving sexual activity. **First degree sexual offense** is discussed in NCGS §14-27.4(a), which states that:

> A person is guilty of a sexual offense in the first degree if the person engages in a sexual act:
> (1) With a victim who is a child under the age of 13 years and the defendant is at least 12 years old and is at least four years older than the victim; or
> (2) With another person by force and against the will of the other person, and:
>   a. Employs or displays a dangerous or deadly weapon or an article which the other person reasonably believes to be a dangerous or deadly weapon; or
>   b. Inflicts serious personal injury upon the victim or another person; or
>   c. The person commits the offense aided and abetted by one or more other persons.

This statute is virtually identical to the one defining first degree rape. The only difference is that the action prohibited is a sexual act, rather than vaginal intercourse. NCGS §14.27.1(4) defines a "sexual act" as:

> cunnilingus, fellatio, analingus, or anal intercourse, but does not include vaginal intercourse. Sexual act also means the penetration, however slight, by any object

26

into the genital or anal opening of another person's body: provided, that it shall be an affirmative defense that the penetration was for accepted medical purposes.

Essentially, the term "sexual act" includes oral sex, anal sex, or the penetration of the victim's body (specifically the genital or anal opening) by some foreign object. It does not include vaginal intercourse, which would elevate the crime to that of rape. Like first degree rape, this crime is a Class B1 felony.

Similarly, the crime of **second degree sexual offense** parallels that of second degree rape. Both are Class C felonies. NCGS §14-27.5(a) states that:

> A person is guilty of a sexual offense in the second degree if the person engages in a sexual act with another person:
> (1) By force and against the will of the other person; or
> (2) Who is mentally disabled, mentally incapacitated, or physically helpless, and the person performing the act knows or should reasonably know that the other person is mentally disabled, mentally incapacitated, or physically helpless.

North Carolina also recognizes the crimes of **statutory rape** and **statutory sexual offense**. These essentially involve non-forcible sexual activities with a minor. **First degree statutory rape** is actually part of the first degree forcible rape statute discussed above. NCGS §14-27.2(a)(1) includes in the crime of first degree rape any vaginal intercourse committed with a child under the age of 13 by a defendant who is at least 12 years of age and at least 4 years older than the victim. **First degree statutory sexual offense** parallels this crime but refers to a sexual act rather than vaginal intercourse.[8]

In addition to these crimes, NCGS §14-27.7A defines the crimes of statutory rape and statutory sexual offense of a person aged 13, 14, or 15 years of age. The statute states that,

> (a) A defendant is guilty of a Class B1 felony if the defendant engages in vaginal intercourse or a sexual act with another person who is 13, 14, or 15 years old and the defendant is at least six years older than the person, except when the defendant is lawfully married to the person.
> (b) A defendant is guilty of a Class C felony if the defendant engages in vaginal intercourse or a sexual act with another person who is 13, 14, or 15 years old and the defendant is more than four but less than six years older than the person, except when the defendant is lawfully married to the person.

This statute essentially defines two different crimes. For the first, and more serious crime, the defendant must be at least six years older than the victim, while for the second offense, the defendant must be more than four but less than six years older than the victim. Age differences are measured from the defendant's birthday to the victim's birthday.

The statute includes a marital exemption, by stating that it is a defense to the crimes of statutory rape and statutory sexual offense that the defendant and the victim are lawfully married. However, marriage is not a defense to the other types of rape and sexual offenses. NCGS §14-27.8 clearly states that:

> A person may be prosecuted under this Article whether or not the victim is the person's legal spouse at the time of the commission of the alleged rape or sexual offense.

In some cases, **consent** may be a defense to a charge under these rape or sexual offense statutes. The age of consent in North Carolina is 16 years of age. An individual under the age of 16 is unable to consent to any vaginal intercourse or sexual act with a person at least four years older. If the victim is at least 16 (and thus legally able to give consent), the statutes (except for statutory rape) all require that the vaginal intercourse or other sexual act be committed without the victim's consent. However, there are some situations where consent may not be used as a defense for intercourse or sexual offenses. These are discussed in NCGS §14-27.7 and include:

- vaginal intercourse or a sexual act with a minor by a defendant who has assumed the position of parent in the minor's home

- vaginal intercourse or a sexual act by a defendant who has custody of the victim (regardless of the victim's age)

- vaginal intercourse or a sexual act by a defendant who is employed by a person or institution that has custody of the victim

- vaginal intercourse or a sexual act by a defendant who is employed as a teacher, school administrator, or coach with a victim who is enrolled as a student at the same school (unless they are lawfully married).

ROBBERY

The FBI's Uniform Crime Reporting Program defines **robbery** as "the taking or attempting to take anything of value from the care, custody, or control of a person or persons by force or threat of force or violence and/or by putting the victim in fear."[9] In North Carolina, robbery is a common law offense. Common law robbery is a Class G felony[10] and includes three elements.[11] The first is that a larceny must be committed. Because larceny is an element of robbery, the state must prove all elements of larceny to be able to convict a defendant of the crime of robbery. The second element is that the larceny must be committed from the person or the presence of the person. This includes taking something from the owner or the owner's control. This element may be satisfied if the object is taken from the body of a homicide victim. Finally, the third element requires the larceny to be committed with violence or intimidation. Actual violence is not required if the victim is placed in fear for his or her immediate physical safety. However, if the only force used is that required to gain possession of the object stolen, and no violence or threat of violence is used to force the victim to relinquish the property, this element is not satisfied. Therefore, a purse snatching in which the only force used is that needed to grab the purse off the shoulder of the victim would not be considered a robbery.[12]

If the robbery was committed with a firearm or other dangerous weapon, the crime is considered to be **armed robbery**, which is a Class D felony. This crime is specifically defined in NCGS §14-87(a), which states that:

> Any person or persons who, having in possession or with the use or threatened use of any firearms or other dangerous weapon, implement or means, whereby the life of a person is endangered or threatened, unlawfully takes or attempts to take personal property from another or from any place of business, residence or banking institution or any other place where there is a person or persons in attendance, at any time, either day or night, or who aids or abets any such person or persons in the commission of such crime, shall be guilty of a Class D felony.

Armed robbery is distinguished from common law robbery by the presence of a firearm or dangerous weapon, which basically is any item that is likely to produce death or great bodily harm. The statute also makes it clear that simple possession of the firearm or weapon is not sufficient to sustain a charge of armed robbery. The weapon must be used in some way that endangers or threatens the life of the victim. Thus, if the offender has a firearm on his or her person but does not use it, display it, or threaten the victim with it, the crime would not be considered armed robbery.

ASSAULT

There is often some confusion about the actual meaning of **assault**. In some states (e.g., Florida, California, Illinois), assault does not actually involve the infliction of an injury upon another person; it is merely an intentional attempt or threat to cause an injury. In these states, when an injury is actually inflicted, a **battery** has occurred. The North Carolina statutes are rather inconsistent. Technically, there is a difference between assault and battery. However, the statutes frequently use the two terms interchangeably, so that the term "assault" may be used in reference to an act that requires striking a victim. Therefore, the term "assault" will be used in this section to include "battery" as well.

The Uniform Crime Reporting Program also considers assault to involve the actual injury of another person. The UCR focuses specifically on aggravated assault, which it defines as:

> an unlawful attack by one person upon another for the purpose of inflicting severe or aggravated bodily injury. This type of assault is usually accompanied by the use of a weapon or by means likely to produce death or great bodily harm.[13]

In North Carolina, **simple assault** is defined by the common law, rather than by statute. It essentially consists of:

> an overt act or attempt, or the unequivocal appearance of attempt, with force and violence, to immediately physically injure another person, with the show of force or menage of violence being sufficient to put a reasonable person in fear of immediate physical injury.[14]

This includes both the physical act of unlawfully touching another person, a battery, as well as the attempt to unlawfully touch the person.

In addition, there are two other types of assault recognized in North Carolina. The first involves **assault by a show of violence** and includes three main elements. The first is that the offender has shown an apparent ability to inflict injury, even if no such ability actually exists. The second is that the act committed by the offender is one that would put a reasonable person in fear of harm. Finally, the third element requires that the act caused the victim to do something that he or she would not otherwise have done. This third element is what distinguishes this type of assault from the regular assault discussed above.

The second type is **assault by criminal negligence**. This type of assault does not require specific intent but occurs when the act that injured the victim resulted from behavior showing a reckless disregard of possible consequences and when physical injury was a foreseeable consequence.

These three types of assault are Class 2 misdemeanors.[15]

NCGS §14-33(c) discusses several types of Class A1 misdemeanor assaults. The statute states that:

> Unless the conduct is covered under some other provision of law providing greater punishment, any person who commits any assault, assault and battery, or affray is guilty of a Class A1 misdemeanor if, in the course of the assault, assault and battery, or affray, he or she:
> (1) Inflicts serious injury upon another person or uses a deadly weapon;
> (2) Assaults a female, he being a male person at least 18 years of age;
> (3) Assaults a child under the age of 12 years;
> (4) Assaults an officer or employee of the State or any political subdivision of the State, when the officer or employee is discharging or attempting to discharge his official duties;
> (5) Repealed by Session Laws 1999-105, s. 1; or
> (6) Assaults a school employee or school volunteer when the employee or volunteer is discharging or attempting to discharge his or her duties as an employee or volunteer, or assaults a school employee or school volunteer as a result of the discharge or attempt to discharge that individual's duties as a school employee or school volunteer.

This statute identifies six different acts that are classified as Class A1 misdemeanor assaults. The first is **assault inflicting serious injury**. This may include either physical or mental injury. The second is **assault with a deadly weapon**, which includes anything that is likely to cause death or serious injury. The third type of assault is **assault of a female**. This category was challenged on the grounds that it violated the Fourteenth Amendment to the U.S. Constitution (the Equal Protection Clause) because a male defendant assaulting a female victim is punished more harshly than a female defendant committing the same action. However, the North Carolina Court of Appeals has held this offense to be constitutional.[16]

The fourth category identified by this statute is **assault of a child under the age of 12**. It is not a defense against this crime that the defendant believed the child was at least 12 years of age. The fifth type of assault is **assault on a governmental officer or employee**. For this crime, the victim may be any local, county, or state government employee or officer. The statute also requires that the victim be discharging or attempting to discharge an official duty. An assault committed because an official duty was discharged is not covered by this crime. Therefore, assaulting a police officer who is attempting to make an arrest would qualify but assaulting the same officer a week later, because of the arrest, would not. Finally, the last type of assault discussed in this statute is **assault on school personnel**. This category includes both employees and volunteers. Unlike the previous category, the statute includes not only assaults on personnel discharging or attempting to discharge official duties but also assaults committed because of those official duties.

In addition, the General Statutes identify several other types of misdemeanor assaults. For example, NCGS §14-34 defines **simple assault by pointing a gun**, stating that, "If any person shall point any gun or pistol at any person, either in fun or otherwise, whether such gun or pistol be loaded or not loaded, he shall be guilty of a Class A1 misdemeanor." NCGS §14-33.2 discusses **habitual misdemeanor assault**, which has three main elements. The offender must have committed one of the six types of assault listed in NCGS 14-33(c) or the crime of assault by pointing a gun, must have at least five prior misdemeanor convictions, and at least two of these prior convictions must have been for assault. This is a Class H felony. If the immediate assault is not one of these seven types (if, for example, the offender committed a felony assault), the offender cannot be charged with habitual misdemeanor assault. In addition, if one of the two prior assault convictions was for a felony assault, the offender would not meet the criteria for this crime.

There are also several other statutes that specifically criminalize assaults committed on specific categories of victims. These include:

- assault with a firearm or other deadly weapon on a governmental officer or employee, a company police officer, or a campus police officer[17]

- assault with a firearm on a law enforcement, probation, or parole officer, or a person employed at a state or local detention facility[18]

- assault inflicting serious injury on a law enforcement, probation, or parole officer, or a person employed at a state or local detention facility[19]

- assault/affray on a firefighter, emergency medical technician, medical responder, or emergency department nurse or doctor[20]

- assault on an executive, legislative, or court officer[21]

- assault on a handicapped person[22]

Some of these are considered to be misdemeanors; others are felonies.

There are several other categories of felonious assault. NCGS §14-32.4 discusses **assault inflicting serious bodily injury**. It is a Class F felony for an offender to assault another person and inflict serious bodily injury on that person. If the offender uses a deadly weapon to commit the assault, the crime is considered to be more serious. NCGS §14-32 defines three types of felony **assault with a deadly weapon**. The first involves an offender who assaults a victim with a deadly weapon and who has intent to kill. This is a Class E felony. An offender who assaults a victim with a deadly weapon and who inflicts serious injury (but who does not have intent to kill) has also committed a Class E felony. Essentially, for the offender to be punished as a Class E felon for assault with a deadly weapon, s/he must either inflict serious injury on the victim or intent to kill the victim, but not both. Finally, if the offender commits an assault with a deadly weapon, inflicts serious injury on the victim, and also has intent to kill, s/he will be punished as a Class C felon.

BURGLARY

The UCR defines burglary as the "unlawful entry of a structure to commit a felony or theft."[23] North Carolina recognizes two levels of burglary, first and second degree. Both are common law crimes. According to NCGS §14-51:

> There shall be two degrees in the crime of burglary as defined at the common law. If the crime be committed in a dwelling house, or in a room used as a sleeping apartment in any building, and any person is in the actual occupation of any part of said dwelling house or sleeping apartment at the time of the commission of such crime, it shall be burglary in the first degree. If such crime be committed in a dwelling house or sleeping apartment not actually occupied by anyone at the time of the commission of the crime, or if it be committed in any house within the curtilage of a dwelling house or in any building not a dwelling house, but in which is a room used as a sleeping apartment and not actually occupied as such at the time of the commission of the crime, it shall be burglary in the second degree. For the purposes of defining the crime of burglary, larceny shall be deemed a felony without regard to the value of the property in question.

First degree burglary is a Class D felony and second degree burglary is a Class G felony.[24]

First degree burglary has eight required elements.[25] These include:

1. Breaking, and
2. Entering
3. Without consent
4. The dwelling house or sleeping apartment room
5. Of another person
6. While the house or room is actually occupied
7. At night
8. With the intent to commit a felony or larceny

All eight elements must be present for the offender to be convicted of first degree burglary. Breaking involves creating an opening in the building. It can be as simple as opening an unlocked door or window. However, if the door or window is already open, the offender has not met the element of breaking. The element of entry is satisfied if the offender puts only a portion of his or her body into the building; it is not necessary for the offender's entire body to be inside the building. The third element is that of lack of consent. For example, if the offender has permission to enter a dwelling, and has been given a key, s/he has not actually met the elements of breaking and entering, even if the offender uses the key to enter the dwelling and commits a felony or larceny. The fourth element refers to the location that is targeted by the offender. For the crime to be a first degree burglary, the target location must be a dwelling or a room used as a sleeping apartment. Target locations that would meet this element include:

- house
- apartment
- condominium
- hotel or motel room
- tent
- mobile home

The fifth element for the crime of burglary requires that the target location must be legally possessed by someone other than the offender. It is possible for an offender to be convicted of burglary of a house he or she owns, if the house is exclusively possessed by someone else. An example would be the owner of a house who has rented the house to a tenant and who opens the door and enters the house without the permission of the tenant. Element six requires the dwelling to be occupied at the time of the crime, although the offender does not have to have had any knowledge of the presence of the occupant. The seventh element relates to the time of the offense: for an offender to be convicted of first degree burglary, the crime must have been committed at night, which means after sunset and before sunrise. Finally, for the crime to be burglary (rather than just breaking and entering), the offender must, while breaking and entering the dwelling, have intent to commit a felony or larceny inside the dwelling. Burglary only requires that the offender intended to commit a larceny or felony. It is not necessary for the prosecution to prove that the defendant actually committed or even attempted to commit the crime to convict. However, if there is no such intent, or if the intent was not formed until after the offender has gained entry to the dwelling, the crime is not burglary. Thus, if the defendant can prove that s/he broke and entered the dwelling for a non-criminal purpose (e.g., to obtain shelter from a storm), the defendant may not be convicted of burglary even if he or she did eventually commit a larceny or felony on the premises, because there was no criminal intent prior to entering the dwelling.

Second degree burglary has seven required elements.[26] These include:

1. Breaking, and
2. Entering
3. Without consent
4. The dwelling house or sleeping apartment room, or any building in the curtilage of the dwelling
5. Of another person
6. At night
7. With the intent to commit a felony or larceny

The elements are very similar to those of first degree burglary but there are two main differences between the two crimes. First of all, the building does not have to be occupied at the time of the crime for a charge of second degree burglary to be sustained. Second, in the crime of second degree burglary, the building targeted for the crime does not have to be a dwelling as long as it is within the curtilage of a dwelling. The statute does not specifically define "curtilage" but this element essentially refers to any building that is close to the dwelling and is regularly used by those living in the dwelling. Examples would be a barn, toolshed, or garage.[27]

The burglary statute clearly limits the location that can be targeted for a burglary (a dwelling for first degree burglary, a dwelling or building within a dwelling's curtilage for second degree burglary). If the target location does not meet these conditions, the crime is not burglary. However, it may be another crime, such as **felonious breaking and entering**. According to NCGS §14-54(a), "Any person who breaks or enters any building with intent to commit any felony or larceny therein shall be punished as a Class H felon." This crime is similar to burglary, but has only four main elements:

1. Breaking or entering
2. Without consent
3. Any building (not just a dwelling)
4. With the intent to commit a felony or larceny within the building[28]

It is not necessary for the offender to both break and enter; either will satisfy the elements of this crime. Thus, while illegally entering through an open door would not satisfy the requirements of burglary, it would satisfy the elements of felonious breaking and entering. As with burglary, the breaking or entering must be done without the consent of the person who possesses the property. Thus, if an offender enters a store during business hours and steals store property, s/he is not guilty of this crime because the owner of the store consented to the entry. However, if the offender enters the store while it is open to the public, remains in the store after closing hours, and then steals store property, s/he would be guilty of this crime.

Finally, NCGS §14-57 specifically discusses the crime of **burglary with explosives**, stating that:

> Any person who, with intent to commit any felony or larceny therein, breaks and enters, either by day or by night, any building, whether inhabited or not, and opens or attempts to open any vault, safe, or other secure place by use of nitroglycerine, dynamite, gunpowder, or any other explosive, or acetylene torch, shall be deemed guilty of burglary with explosives. Any person convicted under this section shall be punished as a Class D felon.

Essentially, this crime requires both breaking and entering of any building (not just a dwelling), at any time of day or night, with intent to commit a felony or larceny, and also requires that the offender uses one of the specific explosives listed in the statute to open or attempt to open a secure place such as a safe or vault. Intent to use explosives is not sufficient to satisfy the is element of the crime; the offender must actually use the explosive device to be convicted of this crime.[29]

LARCENY-THEFT

The FBI defines **larceny-theft** as:

> the unlawful taking, carrying, leading, or riding away of property from the possession or constructive possession of another. It includes crimes such as shoplifting, pocket-picking, purse-snatching, thefts from motor vehicles, thefts of motor vehicle parts and accessories, bicycle thefts, etc., in which no use of force, violence, or fraud occurs.[30]

North Carolina recognizes two main types of larceny: misdemeanor larceny and felony larceny. Both are discussed in NCGS §14-72, which also includes definitions of the crimes of receiving stolen goods and possessing stolen goods (these sections have been deleted for clarity). The statute states that:

> (a) Larceny of goods of the value of more than one thousand dollars ($1,000) is a Class H felony ... Larceny as provided in subsection (b) of this section is a Class H felony ... Except as provided in subsections (b) and (c) of this section, larceny of property ... where the value of the property or goods is not more than one thousand dollars ($1,000), is a Class 1 misdemeanor. In all cases of doubt, the jury shall, in the verdict, fix the value of the property stolen.

(b) The crime of larceny is a felony, without regard to the value of the property in question, if the larceny is:
   (1) From the person; or
   (2) Committed pursuant to a violation of G.S. 14-51, 14-53, 14-54 or 14-57; or
   (3) Of any explosive or incendiary device or substance....
   (4) Of any firearm...
   (5) Of any record or paper in the custody of the North Carolina State Archives as defined by G.S. 121-2(7) and 121-2(8).
(c) ...
(d) Where the larceny ... as described in subsection (a) of this section involves the merchandise of any store, a merchant, a merchant's agent, a merchant's employee, or a peace officer who detains or causes the arrest of any person shall not be held civilly liable for detention, malicious prosecution, false imprisonment, or false arrest of the person detained or arrested, when such detention is upon the premises of the store or in a reasonable proximity thereto, is in a reasonable manner for a reasonable length of time, and, if in detaining or in causing the arrest of such person, the merchant, the merchant's agent, the merchant's employee, or the peace officer had, at the time of the detention or arrest, probable cause to believe that the person committed an offense under subsection (a) of this section. If the person being detained by the merchant, the merchant's agent, or the merchant's employee, is a minor under the age of 18 years, the merchant, the merchant's agent, or the merchant's employee, shall call or notify, or make a reasonable effort to call or notify the parent or guardian of the minor, during the period of detention. A merchant, a merchant's agent, or a merchant's employee, who makes a reasonable effort to call or notify the parent or guardian of the minor shall not be held civilly liable for failing to notify the parent or guardian of the minor.

Based on this statute, **misdemeanor larceny**, a Class 1 misdemeanor, includes five main elements:

1. The offender takes the personal property of another
2. The offender carries the property away
3. The possessor does not consent
4. The offender intends to permanently deprive the possessor of the use of the property
5. The offender knew that s/he was not entitled to the property[31]

The property stolen must be personal property, as opposed to real property. It may include contraband illegally possessed by the victim. The victim does not have to be the owner of the property, s/he must only have legal possession of it at the time of the crime. It is even possible for a defendant who owns property to be convicted of the larceny of that property, if it was in the lawful possession of another person at the time of the crime. The offender must also intend to permanently deprive the victim of the use of the property. Taking property for temporary use does not satisfy this element unless the property was abandoned in such a way that it was unlikely that the possessor would be able to recover it. Finally, the offender must know that s/he is not entitled to the property.

Thus, if the offender honestly believed that s/he had a right to the property, regardless of the truth of this belief, the offender is not guilty of the crime of larceny.

Felony larceny, a Class H felony, is similar to misdemeanor larceny. In addition to the five elements required for misdemeanor larceny, a sixth element must exist. This element requires that any one of six conditions exist.[32] Only one of these conditions is required for a charge of felony larceny to be sustained. The first simply states that the property taken was worth over $1,000. This can include one item with a value of over $1,000 or several items whose value added together totals over $1,000. The second condition is that the larceny was from the person. This means that the property was in the physical possession or within the protection of the person when it was stolen. The third condition includes larceny that was committed pursuant to one of the crimes specified in NCGS §14-72(b)(2). These include burglary, breaking out of a dwelling, breaking or entering a building, or burglary by explosives. The other three conditions refer to specific type of property stolen. It is felony larceny if the property stolen is an explosive or incendiary device, a firearm, or a record or paper in the custody of the North Carolina State Archives.

MOTOR VEHICLE THEFT

The UCR considers **motor vehicle theft** to be a separate index crime from that of theft or larceny-theft. It is defined by the FBI as:

> the theft or attempted theft of a motor vehicle, this offense category includes the stealing of automobiles, trucks, buses, motorcycles, motorscooters, snowmobiles, etc.[33]

Like most states, North Carolina does not separate motor vehicle theft from larceny. In most cases, the theft of a motor vehicle would fall under the crimes of misdemeanor or felony larceny, depending on the value of the vehicle stolen. However, the state also recognizes the crime of **unauthorized use of a motor-propelled conveyance**. NCGS §14-72.2 states that,

> (a) A person is guilty of an offense under this section if, without the express or implied consent of the owner or person in lawful possession, he takes or operates an aircraft, motorboat, motor vehicle, or other motor-propelled conveyance of another.
> (b) Unauthorized use of an aircraft is a Class H felony. All other unauthorized use of a motor-propelled conveyance is a Class 1 misdemeanor.
> (c) Unauthorized use of a motor-propelled conveyance shall be a lesser-included offense of unauthorized use of an aircraft ...

Either taking or operating the vehicle is sufficient to sustain this crime. Thus, if the offender took the vehicle legally but operated it unlawfully (e.g., the offender did not have a license to operate the vehicle), s/he could be convicted of this crime.

This charge is most commonly used for cases of **joyriding**. In these cases, because the offender did not intend to permanently deprive the owner of the vehicle, a charge of larceny would not be sustained.

ARSON

The UCR defines arson as:

> any willful or malicious burning or attempt to burn, with or without intent to defraud, a dwelling house, public building, motor vehicle or aircraft, personal property of another, etc.[34]

Arson in North Carolina is a common law offense. NCGS §14-58 distinguishes between the two levels of arson: first and second degree. First degree arson is a Class D felony while second degree arson is a Class G felony.

First degree arson involves the willful and malicious burning of a dwelling house, or other building within the curtilage of the dwelling, of another person, while someone is present inside the dwelling.[35] The requirement that the crime be committed willfully and maliciously means that the offender intended to burn the dwelling, or that the defendant committed an act that reasonably would result in the burning of the dwelling, and that the act was voluntary and unjustified. The offender must burn the dwelling, but it is not necessary for the dwelling to be destroyed for this element to be met. Damage to some part of the structure is sufficient. The definition also requires that the dwelling burned be possessed by someone other than the offender, or someone in addition to the offender. As with larceny, the key element is possession rather than ownership. If a defendant burns a dwelling that s/he owns but has lawfully rented to another, s/he may be guilty of arson. Finally, for the crime of first degree arson, someone other than the offender must be present in the dwelling at the time of the crime.[36]

Second degree arson is very similar to the crime of first degree arson. The main difference between the two crimes is that it is not necessary for someone to be present inside the dwelling at the time of the burning for the crime of second degree arson to be sustained.[37]

Both types of arson specifically require that the structure burned is a dwelling house or building within the curtilage of the dwelling. NCGS §14-58.1 states that the terms "house" and "building" include "mobile and manufactured-type housing and recreational trailers." For both types of arson, intent is required. A fire that is of accidental or unintentional origin is not considered to be arson.

North Carolina recognizes a number of other crimes that involve the burning of various types of structures other than dwellings. These include:

- burning of certain public buildings[38]

- burning of a schoolhouse or educational institution[39]

- burning of a bridge, fire engine house, rescue squad building, or house owned and used by a corporation or unincorporated association in its business[40]

- burning an uninhabited house, factory, stable, warehouse, office, shop, barn, etc.[41]

- burning a building under construction[42]

- burning a church or other religious building[43]

- burning a boat, barge, ferry, or float[44]

- burning one's own dwelling house for fraudulent purposes[45]

- burning buildings not listed in any other statutes[46]

- burning personal property[47]

HATE CRIMES

Hate or bias crimes are not specifically included among the UCR's eight index crimes. However, the FBI began to collect data on this category of crime after President Bush signed the Hate Crimes Statistics Act in 1990. The UCR defines hate or bias crimes as "those offenses motivated in part or singularly by personal prejudice against others because of a diversity—race, sexual orientation, religion, ethnicity/national origin, or disability.[48]

In North Carolina, the State Bureau of Investigation's Division of Criminal Information collects reports of hate crimes from law enforcement agencies throughout the state. According to the North Carolina Office of the Attorney General, hate crimes are "incidents of violence or crimes perpetrated against persons solely because of their race, religion, national origin/ethnicity or sexual orientation."[49]

There are several statutes that relate specifically to the prosecution of hate crimes. NCGS §14-401.14 states that

(a) If a person shall, because of race, color, religion, nationality, or country of origin, assault another person, or damage or deface the property of another person, or threaten to do any such act, he shall be guilty of a Class 1 misdemeanor.

       (b) A person who assembles with one or more persons to teach any technique or means to be used to commit any act in violation of subsection (a) of this section is guilty of a Class 1 misdemeanor.

In addition, the state allows judges to increase the sentence for any crime that is considered to be a hate crime. According to NCGS §14-3(c), if a Class 2 or 3 misdemeanor was committed because of the race, color, religion, nationality, or country of origin of the victim, the offender will be guilty of a Class 1 misdemeanor. If a Class A1 or 1 misdemeanor was motivated by any of these factors, the offender will be guilty of a Class I felony. NCGS §15A-1340.16(d)(17) states that if any felony was motivated because of the victim's race, color, religion, nationality, or country of origin, this may be considered an aggravating factor by the judge in determining the minimum sentence under the Structured Sentencing Act.

According to the 2000 statistics on crime in North Carolina, 15 agencies in the state reported a total of 39 bias motivated incidents during 2000. Of these, 72 percent were motivated by the race or color of the victim. Other motivations included the victim's ethnicity or national origin (18 percent), religion (8 percent), and sexual orientation (3 percent).[50]

NOTES

1.   Recent issues of the *Uniform Crime Reports* may be viewed online on the Federal Bureau of Investigation's website (http://www.fbi.gov/ucr/ucr.htm)
2.   *Uniform Crime Reports* (http://www.fbi.gov/ucr/ucr.htm)
3.   Farb, Robert L., ed. (2001). *North Carolina Crimes: A Guidebook on the Elements of Crime.* Chapel Hill, N.C.: University of North Carolina at Chapel Hill Institute of Government.
4.   North Carolina General Statutes, §14-18
5.   Farb, R.L. *op. cit.*
6.   *Uniform Crime Reports, op. cit.*
7.   *State v. Murry*, 277 N.C. 197, 176 S.E.2d 738 (1970).
8.   North Carolina General Statutes, §14.27.4(a)(1)
9.   *Uniform Crime Reports, op cit.*
10.   North Carolina General Statutes, §14-87.1
11.   Farb, R.L. *op. cit.*
12.   *Ibid*
13.   *Uniform Crime Reports, op. cit.*
14.   Farb, R.L. *op. cit.* p.80
15.   North Carolina General Statutes, §14-33(a)
16.   *State of North Carolina vs. Robinson*, 39 N.C. App. 395
17.   North Carolina General Statutes, §14-34.2
18.   North Carolina General Statutes, §14-34.5
19.   North Carolina General Statutes, §14-34.7
20.   North Carolina General Statutes, §14-34.6
21.   North Carolina General Statutes, §14-16.6

22. North Carolina General Statutes, §14-32.1
23. *Uniform Crime Reports, op. cit.*
24. North Carolina General Statutes, §14-52
25. Farb, R.L. *op. cit.*
26. *Ibid*
27. *Ibid*
28. *Ibid*
29. *Ibid*
30. *Uniform Crime Reports, op. cit.*
31. Farb, R.L., *op. cit.*
32. North Carolina General Statutes, §14-72
33. *Uniform Crime Reports, op. cit.*
34. *Ibid*
35. Farb, R.L., *op. cit.*
36. North Carolina General Statutes, §14-58
37. *Ibid*
38. North Carolina General Statutes, §14-59
39. North Carolina General Statutes, §14-60
40. North Carolina General Statutes, §14-61
41. North Carolina General Statutes, §14-62
42. North Carolina General Statutes, §14-62.1
43. North Carolina General Statutes, §14-62.2
44. North Carolina General Statutes, §14-63
45. North Carolina General Statutes, §14-65
46. North Carolina General Statutes, §14-67.1
47. North Carolina General Statutes, §14-66
48. Recent issues of the FBI's *Hate Crime Statistics* may be viewed online on the FBI's website (http://www.fbi.gov/ucr/ucr.htm)
49. Office of the Attorney General home page (http://www.jus.state.nc.us/)
50. Crime in North Carolina, 2000 (http://sbi2.jus.state.nc.us/crp/public/Default.htm)

CHAPTER 4

THE POLICE IN NORTH CAROLINA

INTRODUCTION

There are many levels of police agencies in America today, including federal law enforcement, state police, county sheriff's agencies, and city police. Currently, there are over 500 separate law enforcement agencies in North Carolina. Most of these are municipal or city departments, each of which has its own chief, its own organization, and its own policies and procedures. In 2002, there were a total of 379 separate municipal police departments in North Carolina.[1] In addition, there are 100 county sheriff's departments, the North Carolina State Highway Patrol, and a wide variety of special-purpose law enforcement agencies at all levels of government. Currently, there are approximately 30,000 certified law enforcement officers in North Carolina.

LOCAL POLICING

The majority of the police departments in North Carolina are local or city departments. Currently, there are 379 separate local police agencies in the state. In most cases, the chief of each department is appointed by the head of the city's political system (city manager, mayor, commissioner, etc.) Because of this, it can be a very political position. If a new city manager is elected, the appointment of a new police chief often follows soon afterwards. Every local department is independent of every other department. The goals, purposes, and priorities vary greatly among departments, with each local agency responding to the needs and desires of the population it serves. All municipal police departments are full-service police agencies which provide a wide range of police services, including law enforcement, order maintenance, and service. According to the North Carolina Criminal Justice Education and Training Standards Commission, there were 13,449 certified police officers employed in local police departments in North Carolina in 2002.[2]

The Durham Police Department

Durham is located in the Piedmont region of the state and has a population of almost 200,000 individuals. The **Durham Police Department** (DPD) has 476 sworn officers and 92 civilian employees.[3] Currently, the minimum entry requirements for the department include:

- be 21 years of age by the completion of academy classroom training
- be a US citizen
- completion of high school or equivalent (GED) with some college preferred
- meet departmental vision, hearing, and physical requirements
- no felony convictions
- no domestic violence convictions
- no serious misdemeanor convictions in the past five years

- no DWI or DUI convictions in the past 10 years
- have a valid driver's license
- no suspensions of driving privileges in th past three years
- meet departmental credit history requirements

Applicants who meet these requirements must go through a variety of tests, including a written examination, physical fitness tests, a medical examination, behavioral and psychological assessments, a background investigation, polygraph and drug screening tests, and an oral review. Recruits then attend a 23-week police academy training program (seven weeks longer than the 16-week minimum training period required by the state), studying a wide variety of subjects including North Carolina law and rules of evidence, the laws of arrest, search and seizure, patrol techniques, firearm techniques, pursuit driving, defensive techniques, intensive "survival Spanish", diversity training, and first aid. Academy graduates then go through an on-the job field training program, working with experienced officers. Base salaries start at $30,060, with an increase to $33,039 upon completion of the full training program. There are a variety of additional pay and bonus opportunities within the department.[4]

The Greensboro Police Department

Greensboro is located in the Piedmont region of the state and has a population of over 225,000 persons. The **Greensboro Police Department** (GPD) was founded in 1889 and currently has 511 sworn officers and 176 civilian employees.[5] In 1987, the GPD became the first department in North Carolina to achieve "Accreditation" status from the Commission on Accreditation for Law Enforcement Agencies (CALEA).

One of the more unique programs at the GPD is the **Student Outreach and Recruiting Program** (SOAR) which focuses on high school students who show an interest in police work. It began as a common Police Explorer program but, in 1999, the program was expanded into a cadet program including education and on-the-job training as a way of preparing high school students for future employment with the GPD. High school students are given the opportunity to take criminal justice courses at the Guilford Technical Community College (GTCC) and up to 15 new SOAR participants are recruited each year from those who take the basic criminology course at the college. Participants may be eligible for scholarships to GTCC upon completion of the program. SOAR students must maintain a 2.0 grade point average and a good school attendance record, and may not have committed any crimes or other actions that would disqualify them from becoming a GPD police officer. Participants attend meetings twice a month, participate in fundraising activities and monthly community service projects, and attend a summer camp between junior and senior years of high school. During the second year of participation in the program, SOAR members work five (paid) hours per week in the GPD during the school year.

Currently, the minimum entry requirements for the GPD include:

- be a U.S. citizen
- be a high school graduate or the equivalent (G.E.D. certificate)
- be at least 21 years of age upon completion of academy training
- no felony convictions

44

- no serious misdemeanor convictions
- meet departmental physical requirements
- be able to obtain a valid North Carolina driver's licence

Applicants who meet the minimum requirements go through a variety of tests, including a written examination, background investigation, medical, psychological, and poloygraph examinations, drug screening, and an oral board interview. Starting salary levels are determined by the officer's level of educational achievement. New recruits go through a 20-week academy training program, followed by 14 weeks of on-the-job field training. A new officer with a high school diploma or GED earned a starting salary of $31,500 in 2002. An officer with an AA degree started at a salary of $33,075, while an officer with a BA or BS degree earned a starting salary of $34,650. Officers are eligible for promotion and/or transfer to specialized units after two years with the department.[6]

Unlike the DPD, the GPD accepts lateral entry police officers. This means that police officers currently certified in North Carolina may apply for a transfer to the GPD at their current rank. Lateral entry applicants must meet certain qualifications, including:

- must be a certified law enforcement officer in North Carolina
- must have served two consecutive years in patrol with their current law enforcement agency, provided that the agency is in North Carolina
- must be able to meet the physical requirements of the job
- must have a high school education or the equivalent
- must successfully pass written, medical, and polygraph examinations, a psychological interview, and a background investigation

As with entry level officers, the officer's level of educational achievement determines entry level salary. Lateral entry officers serve a period of one year on probation, after which they are eligible for transfer to a specialized unit or for promotion to the rank of corporal. They are eligible for promotion to the rank of sergeant after four years with the GPD.[7]

COUNTY POLICING

Each of the 100 counties in North Carolina has a separate sheriff's department. The office of sheriff is mandated by the North Carolina Constitution, which states that,

> In each county a Sheriff shall be elected by the qualified voters thereof at the same
> time and places as members of the General Assembly are elected and shall hold his
> office for a period of four years, subject to removal for cause as provided by law.[8]

These requirements are repeated in NCGS §162-1. In addition, NCGS §162-2 outlines several disqualifications for the office, stating that:

> No person shall be eligible for the office of sheriff who is not of the age of 21 years,
> or has not resided in the county in which he is chosen for one year immediately

preceding his election. No person shall engage in the practice of law or serve as a member of the General Assembly while serving as sheriff.

Other than this, the statutes do not set forth any other legal minimum requirements to be met by candidates running for the office of sheriff.

Sheriff's departments in North Carolina are full service police agencies that provide police services to all unincorporated areas of the county. In addition, incorporated cities that do not wish to set up their own city police department may contract out to their county sheriff's department for police services. Chapter 162, Article 3 of the General Statutes describes the duties of sheriffs in North Carolina. Not only is the sheriff responsible for providing law enforcement services to the county, but s/he is also responsible for executing various civil and criminal processes, executing summons, orders, and judgments, and running the county jail.

According to the North Carolina Sheriffs' Education and Training Standards Commission, in 2002 there were a total of 11,527 certified sheriffs' deputies and 7,181 certified detention officers in the state of North Carolina.[9]

The Mecklenberg County Sheriff's Office

The **Mecklenberg County Sheriff's Office** (MCSO) serves the county with the largest population in the state of North Carolina. It is responsible for providing services to the citizens of Mecklenberg County in the areas of law enforcement, courts, and corrections (the jail). Mecklenberg County has had a county sheriff since at least 1770 (possibly earlier). Sheriffs were appointed until 1829, when the statutes were changed to require the election of sheriffs by popular vote. During much of the 19th century, the MCSO provided all law enforcement services in the county. However, in 1865, the county's first municipal department, the Town of Charlotte Police Department, was established. This left the MCSO primarily responsible for providing law enforcement services to rural areas of the county.

Currently, the MCSO is the third largest law enforcement agency in the state. It has a budget of nearly $77 million and employs almost 1,250 employees. It is divided into a number of divisions. The **Civil Division** is responsible for serving a wide variety of legal papers, including civil summons, magistrate summons, subpoenas, notices of hearing, domestic violence protective orders, and temporary restraining orders. Deputies assigned to the **Court Services Division** serve as court bailiffs and provide security for county courthouses. The **Detention Division** is responsible for the county jail system, which consists of three main facilities: Jail-Central (a pre-trial detention and intake facility), Jail-North (a facility for sentenced offenders), and the Work Release and Restitution Center.

Currently, the minimum entry requirements necessary to be considered for employment as a deputy sheriff by the MCSO include:

- a minimum age of 21
- U.S. citizen
- no felony convictions
- no convictions for Class B misdemeanors in the past five years

- no convictions for Class A misdemeanors within the past three years and no more than two such convictions in a lifetime
- no convictions for DWI within the past five years and no more than one such conviction in a lifetime
- high school graduate or the equivalent
- possess or be able to obtain a valid North Carolina driver's license
- have no more than four suspensions or revocations of a driver's license in a lifetime
- live within 50 miles of Jail-Central
- excellent physical condition
- pass a physical examination
- pass a background investigation
- weight proportionate to height and body frame
- vision correctable to 20/20 in both eyes
- normal color vision (no color blindness)
- meet all training and testing performance standards required by the North Carolina Sheriffs' Education and Training Standards Commission

The starting salary for a deputy sheriff with MCSO is $28,300.[10]

The Wake County Sheriff's Office

Wake County is one of the largest counties in North Carolina. It is known as the "Capital County" because Raleigh, the capital of the state, is located in central Wake County. The **Wake County Sheriff's Office** (WCSO) is responsible for providing a wide variety of services in the areas of law enforcement, court services, detention, and service of civil processes. A total of 480 personnel are employed in the WCSO, which is divided into five main divisions: Patrol, Investigative, Administrative, Judicial Services, and Detention.

To be eligible for a position as deputy sheriff with WCSO, applicants must meet the following minimum requirements:

- be at least 21 years of age
- be a US citizen
- be a high school graduate or the equivalent
- have no criminal history
- have a good driving record
- undergo an extensive background investigation
- complete basic training during the first year of employment
- live in Wake County if hired

The starting salary depends on the employee's background. For example, an applicant who only meets the minimum requirements will earn the base salary of $29,705. Applicants with a two-year college degree or who have military service will earn 3 percent above the base salary, starting at $30,600, while applicants with a four-year college degree will start at $31,490 (six percent above base). Applicants who are already certified and have some experience may also earn above-base salaries.[11]

STATE POLICING

There are two main types of **state police agencies** within the United States. Some states, such as Pennsylvania, operate a **centralized** or full-service state police agency which includes both highway patrol functions and criminal investigation. However, other states, such as North Carolina, separate or **decentralize** the functions and keep criminal investigations separate from the uniformed highway patrol. In 2002, there were a total of 3,678 certified law enforcement officers employed in North Carolina state law enforcement agencies.[12]

The North Carolina Department of Crime Control and Public Safety

The **North Carolina Department of Crime Control and Public Safety** (CCPS) is a statewide agency that serves as the main public safety department for the state. It was created in 1977 by an act of the General Assembly and merges key public safety agencies together into one department. The responsibilities of CCPS agencies include not only to enforce state laws but also to assist local agencies in crime prevention, to provide aid to crime victims, to serve as the state's emergency response coordinator during natural and manmade emergencies (hurricanes, tropical storms, tornados, major snowstorms, chemical spills, etc.), to direct statewide relief efforts for disaster victims, and to serve as the state's Office of Homeland Security. The divisions and commissions that comprise the CCPS include:

- North Carolina Alcohol Law Enforcement Division
- North Carolina Boxing Commission
- Butner Public Safety Division
- Civil Air Patrol Division
- Division of Emergency Management
- Governor's Crime Commission
- Law Enforcement Support Services
- North Carolina National Guard
- North Carolina State Highway Patrol
- Victim Compensation Services Division

In October 2002, the General Assembly ratified a bill that merged the Division of Motor Vehicles (DMV) with the North Carolina State Highway Patrol, bringing DMV enforcement under the umbrella of the CCPS. The merger took place effective January 1, 2003, when the uniformed division of the DMV was transferred from the Department of Transportation to the CCPS. These officers became members of a new section of the Highway Patrol, although they will continue to function as DMV officers and, at least in the short term, will retain their DMV uniforms, equipment, and vehicles.

The North Carolina State Highway Patrol

The **North Carolina State Highway Patrol** (North Carolina HP) is a division of the CCPS.[13] It was created in 1929, by an act of the General Assembly, after it was realized that the number of vehicles registered in the state, and the number of individuals killed in traffic accidents, were increasing. The Highway Patrol was responsible for enforcing motor vehicle laws, patrolling state highways, and assisting the "motoring public." Of the 67 men selected to participate in the first training school class in May 1929, 42 completed the course and 37 were selected to serve in the Highway Patrol. The patrol was officially activated on July 1, 1929. The first member of the patrol was killed the following day, while riding a motorcycle to his assigned duty station. Original monthly salaries were $150 for patrolmen, $175 for lieutenants, and $200 for commanders. However, salary reductions occurred repeatedly and, by 1935, the monthly salary for a patrolman was only $87.50.

Originally, the patrol had nine highway districts, each with one lieutenant and three patrolmen. All patrolmen drove Harley Davidson motorcycles, while the lieutenants and the patrol commander drove automobiles. The state headquarters for the patrol was located in Raleigh. The size of the patrol increased to 67 members in 1931 and to 121 members in 1933. Their responsibilities increased to include issuing drivers' licenses and enforcing new drivers' license laws. Over the years there have been many more changes in duties and responsibilities, as well as in the rank and organizational structure of the patrol.[14]

According to NCGS §20-188, the duties of the North Carolina HP require them to,

> regularly patrol the highways of the State and enforce all laws and regulations
> respecting travel and the use of vehicles upon the highways of the State and all laws
> for the protection of the highways of the State.

Members of the North Carolina HP have statewide jurisdiction and have the authority of any police officer with respect to making arrests for crimes committed on any highways in the state.[15]

Currently, the North Carolina HP has six sections: Administrative Services; Communications and Logistics; Inspection and Internal Affairs; Research and Planning; Training; and Zone Operations (the patrol's enforcement arm). The North Carolina HP is involved in a variety of activities. One area of focus is that of drug seizure. In 2001, the patrol seized over 3,300 grams of cocaine, over 1.4 million grams of marijuana, and over $230,000 in currency. The patrol also focuses on a variety of traffic violations, including violations of child restraint laws, seat belt violations, driving while impaired, and speeding. In 2001, the patrol also investigated over 98,000 reportable traffic collisions.[16]

The North Carolina State Bureau of Investigation

The **North Carolina State Bureau of Investigation** (SBI) is part of the Department of Justice and is responsible for assisting local and county law enforcement agencies with a variety of criminal investigations. The SBI has limited jurisdiction in crimes such as homicides, robberies, property crimes, and missing persons. The local department must request the SBI's assistance, and original jurisdiction over the case remains with the originating department. Requests for assistance come from police chiefs, sheriffs, fire marshals, district attorneys, judges, the state attorney general, and the governor of North Carolina. The SBI also has original jurisdiction over drug and arson investigations, misuse or theft of state property, investigations into child abuse in day care centers, and violations of state election laws.

The SBI was originally known as the State Bureau of Identification and Investigation and was created by an act of the General Assembly in 1937 and became operational in 1938. According to NCGS §114-12, the SBI was created to "secure a more effective administration of the criminal laws of the State, to prevent crime, and to procure the speedy apprehension of criminals..." The name was changed to the State Bureau of Investigation in 1939 and the agency was placed in the Department of Justice under the authority of the Attorney General. Members of the SBI have the same powers of arrest as sheriffs and have statewide jurisdiction.[17] Other statutory responsibilities of the SBI include maintaining criminal laboratory facilities to assist local agencies with the examination and analysis of criminal evidence[18] and the collection, organization, and dissemination of criminal statistics.[19]

One of the SBI's main areas of focus is drug investigations, over which the agency has original jurisdiction. The agency works with a variety of local departments and federal agencies in an effort to stop illegal drugs moving in and out of the state. The SBI's **Clandestine Laboratory Program** focuses on the illegal manufacture of controlled substances. The **Drug Interdiction Program** conducts investigations throughout the state, attempting to identify drug couriers and prevent the movement of illegal drugs. The **Marijuana Eradication Program** attempts to locate and eradicate illegally grown marijuana in North Carolina.[20]

POLICE TRAINING

Police departments today require highly-qualified and well-trained officers. In 1971, the General Assembly created the **North Carolina Criminal Justice Education and Training Standards Commission**. The Assembly stated,

> that the administration of criminal justice is of statewide concern, and that proper administration is important to the health, safety and welfare of the people of the State and is of such nature as to require education and training of a professional nature. It is in the public interest that such education and training be made available to persons who seek to become criminal justice officers, persons who are serving as such officers in a temporary or probationary capacity, and persons already in regular service.[21]

The Assembly gave the Commission the authority to establish minimum educational and training standards for law enforcement and other criminal justice officers, and minimum standards for the certification of training programs for criminal justice officers.[22]

The Commission sets minimum employment standards for police officers in North Carolina. According to the Commission, an individual wishing to qualify for certification must:

- be a citizen of the United States;

- be at least 20 years of age;

- be of good moral character as verified through a background investigation;

- have been fingerprinted and a search made of fingerprint files for any record;

- not have committed or been convicted of a felony, serious misdemeanor or several less serious misdemeanors;

- be a high school graduate or have passed the General Educational Development (GED) Test;

- have completed a Commission-accredited Basic Law Enforcement Training (BLET) course and the employing agency's in-service firearms training program;

- have been examined and certified by a licensed physician as fit to perform the duties of a police officer;

- have been interviewed by the department head or his/her representative to determine suitability;

- have produced a negative result on a drug screen administered according to the specifications established by the Commission; and have been administered a psychological screening examination by a clinical psychologist or psychiatrist to determine mental and emotional suitability.[23]

These are minimum requirements. Any law enforcement agency may establish qualifications for employment that exceed these minimum requirements. For example, both the Durham and Greensboro Police Departments require applicants to be at least 21 years of age upon completion of basic academy training.[24]

In 1983, the General Assembly created the **North Carolina Sheriffs' Education and Training Standards Commission**. The Assembly felt that,

> the office of sheriff, the office of deputy sheriff and the other officers and employees of the sheriff of a county are unique among all of the law-enforcement offices of North Carolina. The administration of criminal justice has been declared by Chapter 17C of the General Statutes to be of statewide concern to the people of the State. The sheriff is the only officer of local government required by the Constitution. The sheriff, in addition to his criminal justice responsibilities, is the only officer who is also responsible for the courts of the State, and acting as their bailiff and marshall. The sheriff administers and executes criminal and civil justice and acts as the ex officio detention officer.
>
> The deputy sheriff has been held by the Supreme Court of this State to hold an office of special trust and confidence, acting in the name of and with powers coterminous with his principal, the elected sheriff.
>
> The offices of sheriff and deputy sheriff are therefore of special concern to the public health, safety, welfare and morals of the people of the State. The training and educational needs of such officers therefore require particularized and differential treatment from those of the criminal justice officers certified under Chapter 17C of the General Statutes.[25]

51

In other words, the Assembly felt that a separate Commission was necessary for the development of minimum education and training standards of sheriffs. The Sheriff's Commission is responsible for certifying all deputy sheriffs, detention officers, and telecommunications officers who work in sheriffs' departments in North Carolina. The Sheriff's Commission also sets minimum employment standards and develops training programs. North Carolina is unique in the United States as the only state that has two regulatory agencies responsible for responsible for setting minimum employment, training, and certification standards for law enforcement personnel in the state. It is possible for a law enforcement officer to hold multiple certifications and to come under the responsibility of both Commissions.[26]

Individuals wishing to become a certified law enforcement officer in North Carolina must go through a **Basic Law Enforcement Training** program (BLET). The BLET course includes a variety of topics, including firearms, search and seizure, arrest, law (including criminal, constitutional, motor vehicle, ABC, and juvenile law), patrol techniques, driver training, criminal and traffic investigation, traffic enforcement, civil processes, domestic violence response, crime prevention physical fitness, first responder techniques, and ethics. It is a 16-week, 602 hour course that includes both classroom work and practical exercises. There are over 70 sites in the state that are authorized and accredited to offer the BLET course, including the SBI, the North Carolina HP, a number of police departments, and various community colleges.[27]

THE NORTH CAROLINA POLICE CORPS

The federal **Police Corps Program** is

> designed to address violent crime by helping state and local law enforcement agencies increase the number of officers with advanced education and training assigned to community patrol. The program, which operates within states that have submitted an approved state plan, motivates highly qualified young people to serve as police officers and sheriffs' deputies in the municipalities, counties and states that need them most. It does this by offering Federal scholarships on a competitive basis to college students who agree to serve where needed on community patrol for at least four years.
>
> The Police Corps reduces local costs of hiring and training excellent new officers. The Federal government pays for rigorous law enforcement training for each Police Corps participant...[28]

Police Corps participants generally spend all four years of their service commitment on community patrol. They have all the same rights and responsibilities as any other member of their agency and receive the same pay and benefits.

North Carolina has been involved in the Police Corps since 1996 and was one of the first states to develop a state program. The **North Carolina Police Corps** is designed to attract individuals to the field of policing in the state of North Carolina. The undergraduate police corps program focuses on high school seniors as well as full-time college students enrolled in a four-year college or university and provides scholarships towards tuition, room, board, and other expenses. After graduating from college, the participant attends a 24-week residential training program and receives a monthly stipend of $1,450, along with room, board, and uniforms. After completing the training program, the participant is committed to serve four years with an assigned law enforcement agency in the state.

The graduate police corps program is designed for college graduates who want to attend graduate school after completing their four-year service commitment. These participants go through the residential training program, serve four years with an assigned agency, and then receive scholarships towards the cost of graduate school.[29]

NOTES

1. North Carolina Criminal Justice Education and Training Standards Commission home page (http://www.jus.state.nc.us/otsmain/CJWeb/CJwhat.htm)
2. *Ibid*
3. Durham Police Department home page (http://www.durhampolice.com/)
4. *Ibid*
5. Greensboro Police Department home page (http://www.ci.greensboro.nc.us/police/)
6. *Ibid*
7. *Ibid*
8. North Carolina Constitution, Article VIII, §2
9. Mr. Benjamin Morris, North Carolina Sheriffs' Education and Training Standards Commission, personal communication, April 30, 2003
10. Mecklenberg County Sheriff's Office home page (http://www.charmeck.org/Departments/MCSO/Home.htm)
11. Wake County Sheriff's Office home page (http://rtpnet.org/~wcso/index.html)
12. North Carolina Criminal Justice Education and Training Standards Commission home page, *op. cit.*
13. North Carolina General Statutes, §20-184
14. North Carolina State Highway Patrol home page (http://www.ncshp.org/)
15. North Carolina General Statutes, §20-188
16. North Carolina State Highway Patrol home page, *op. cit.*
17. North Carolina General Statutes, §114-14
18. North Carolina General Statutes, §114-16
19. North Carolina General Statutes, §114-19
20. North Carolina State Bureau of Investigation home page (http://sbi.jus.state.nc.us/sbimain/ncsbi.htm)
21. North Carolina General Statutes, §17C-1
22. North Carolina General Statutes, §17C-6
23. North Carolina Criminal Justice Education and Training Standards Commission home page, *op. cit.*
24. Durham Police Department home page and Greensboro Police Department home page, *op. cit.*
25. North Carolina General Statutes, §17E-1

26. North Carolina Sheriffs' Education and Training Standards Commission home page (http://www.jus.state.nc.us/otsmain/sheriffs/index.htm)
27. North Carolina Justice Academy home page (http://www.jus.state.nc.us/NCJA/)
28. Office of the Police Corps home page (http://www.ojp.usdoj.gov/opclee/)
29. NC Police Corps home page (http://www.jus.state.nc.us/NCJA/pcorps.htm)

CHAPTER 5

THE COURT SYSTEM IN NORTH CAROLINA

INTRODUCTION

The court system in North Carolina is known as the General Court of Justice. The North Carolina State Constitution divides the General Court into three divisions, an appellate division, a superior court division, and a district court division[1]. The superior and district courts are the trial courts of the state. The appellate division has two levels of courts: the Supreme Court and the Court of Appeals.[2]

The court system in North Carolina became a unified state-operated court system in 1966. Prior to that time, the state operated the supreme and superior courts but the lower courts were operated by cities or counties. As a result, the jurisdiction of the lower courts was not uniform across the state, but varied by county. In the 1950s, the North Carolina Bar Association formed the **Committee on Improving and Expediting the Administration of Justice in North Carolina**, also known as the "Bell Commission", after its chairman, J. Spencer Bell. After studying the court system, the commission's recommendation to the General Assembly was that the state judicial system needed to be completely restructured. In 1962, the voters approved an amendment to the North Carolina State Constitution that created the current judicial system, which became operational in 1966. Changes included the development of the Court of Appeals, an intermediate appellate court, and the development of a uniform district court system to replace a wide variety of city and county courts.[3]

FEDERAL COURTS IN NORTH CAROLINA

There are a number of federal courts which sit in North Carolina. These should not be confused with the state trial and appellate courts.

Although they are not specifically part of the North Carolina State Court system, there are three **federal district courts** which sit in North Carolina[4]. These are the Eastern District Court, the Middle District Court, and the Western District Court. They are the trial courts of the federal system, and are not related to the state district courts.

The **U.S. Courts of Appeals** are the intermediate appellate court of the federal court system and have appellate jurisdiction only over federal laws. Judges in these courts are nominated by the President of the United States and confirmed by the Senate. North Carolina, along with Maryland, South Carolina, Virginia, and West Virginia, is part of the Fourth Circuit[5]. The U.S. Court of Appeals is not related to the state court of appeal, although they are both appellate courts.

THE NORTH CAROLINA SUPREME COURT

The **Supreme Court of North Carolina** is the state's highest court, and there is no further appeal in the state from the decisions of this court. Its decisions are binding upon all other courts in the state.

According to the North Carolina State Constitution, the Supreme Court is made up of seven justices, including a chief justice and six associate justices. However, the General Assembly has the right to add up to two additional associate justices.[6] Four justices make up a quorum for the purposes of transacting court business.[7] All Supreme Court justices are elected by the qualified voters of the state and serve eight-year terms.[8] To serve as a Supreme Court justice, an individual must be authorized to practice law in North Carolina state courts.[9] In addition, NCGS §7A-4.20 states that no judges or justices may continue to serve past the last day of the month in which they reach their 72nd birthday (although on occasion, retired judges and justices may be recalled for temporary service). The North Carolina Supreme Court sits in the Supreme Court Building in Raleigh.

The North Carolina State Constitution outlines the jurisdiction of the Court, stating that:

> The Supreme Court shall have jurisdiction to review upon appeal any decision of the courts below, upon any matter of law or legal inference. The jurisdiction of the Supreme Court over "issues of fact" and "questions of fact" shall be the same exercised by it prior to the adoption of this Article, and the Court may issue any remedial writs necessary to give it general supervision and control over the proceedings of the other courts. The Supreme Court also has jurisdiction to review, when authorized by law, direct appeals from a final order or decision of the North Carolina Utilities Commission.[10]

The General Assembly has expanded upon this in the General Statutes, describing both the original and appellate jurisdiction of the Supreme Court. NCGS §7A-25 discusses the original jurisdiction of the Supreme Court, stating that:

> The Supreme Court has original jurisdiction to hear claims against the State, but its decisions shall be merely recommendatory; no process in the nature of execution shall issue thereon; the decisions shall be reported to the next session of the General Assembly for its action. The court shall by rule prescribe the procedures to be followed in the proper exercise of the jurisdiction conferred by this section.

The Supreme Court also has appellate jurisdiction over decisions of the lower courts of the General Court of Justice.[11] The Court's appellate responsibilities include both mandatory and discretionary reviews. Mandatory review, which is known as an **appeal of right**, includes those cases which the Court is required by law to hear, such as reviews of any case of first degree murder in which the defendant receives a sentence of death.[12] Discretionary reviews involve those cases in which the Court chooses to review decisions of the Court of Appeals, although this review is not required. The Supreme Court does not make determinations of fact upon appeal but focuses on errors in legal procedures and on judicial interpretations of state laws. In addition to reviewing all death penalty cases, the Court focuses primarily on cases that involve issues of constitutional law and significant legal questions.

The Court also has the authority to issue certain types of writs, which are orders requiring a person to perform a particular act or to refrain from performing a particular act. The Court may issue a variety of writs, including writs of *habeas corpus*, *mandamus*, prohibition, *certiorari*, and *supersedeas*.[13] Decisions of the North Carolina Supreme Court are published in the *North Carolina Reports*.

THE NORTH CAROLINA COURT OF APPEALS

North Carolina Court of Appeals is the state's intermediate appellate court of review. Prior to its creation in 1967, all appeals were heard by the Supreme Court. However, increasing problems of delay and congestion within the Supreme Court led to the development of the current two-tier appellate court system, with the Court of Appeals acting as a "buffer" between the lower trial courts and the North Carolina Supreme Court. By handling the majority of the appellate work in the state, the Court of Appeals allows the Supreme Court to review only those cases that raise important legal questions and to ensure that decisions made throughout the state are uniform. Today, the majority of cases which are appealed from the superior and district courts do not reach the North Carolina Supreme Court but are reviewed by the Court of Appeals.

The North Carolina State Constitution has left the structure, organization, and composition of the Court of Appeals for the General Assembly to determine, although it does mandate that the Court of Appeals must have at least five members.[14] Currently, the Court of Appeals has fifteen judges, who sit in rotating panels of three. Like Supreme Court justices, judges of the Court of Appeals are elected by the voters and serve eight-year terms.[15] The requirements to serve as a Court of Appeals judge are the same as for a Supreme Court justice. During the 2000-2001 fiscal year, over 1,500 cases were filed with the court.[16]

In most cases the court sits in Raleigh, but it may sit in other locations around the state. Like the Supreme Court, the Court of Appeals focuses on questions of law rather than on determinations of fact. The Court of Appeals hears all appeals from trial courts except for those cases that are directly appealable to the Supreme Court. Decisions are based on the merits of the case, using the record from the original trial court; the Court of Appeals does not hear additional testimony or retry the case. In most cases, the decision of the Court of Appeals represents the final appellate review of a litigated case and is therefore final, although further appeals may be made to either the North Carolina Supreme Court or the U.S. Supreme Court.

Cases move from the Court of Appeals to the North Carolina Supreme Court in one of two ways. Cases in which there is a dissent in the Court of Appeals, and those cases that involve questions of constitutional law go to the Supreme Court from the Court of Appeals by right. This means that the party appealing the case has a right to have it heard by the appellate court. All other cases that are appealed go to the appellate division by certification. This means that the Supreme Court makes a decision whether or not to review a case that has been decided by the Court of Appeals. In some cases, the Supreme Court may decide to bypass the Court of Appeals and hear a case directly. The Supreme Court is not required to review a case that is appealed by certification and the majority of such appeals are denied.[17]

THE NORTH CAROLINA SUPERIOR COURT DIVISION

According to NCGS §7A-40, "The Superior Court Division of the General Court of Justice consists of the several superior courts of the State." The state is divided into eight judicial divisions, which are further divided into superior court districts, each with a specified number of resident judges.[18]

The **superior court** is the court of general trial jurisdiction in North Carolina. This court hears all felony criminal cases, all civil cases that involve over $10,000, and all appeals upon conviction from a district court that involve misdemeanors and infractions. Criminal trials in superior court are heard by a jury of twelve. Civil trials may also have a 12-person jury but in these cases the right to a trial by jury is frequently waived. Unlike appeals made to the appellate division, which are decided on issues of law, defendants who appeal criminal cases from the district to superior court receive a *trial de novo,* or a completely new trial. Approximately one-third of all criminal cases heard by the superior court are misdemeanor cases on appeal from the district court.

The superior court division has a total of 91 judges, who are assigned to specific judicial divisions. These judges are elected by the voters of their superior court district.[19] Superior court judges are required to live in the district in which they are elected.[20] Every six months, judges rotate among the districts within their division. By not having judges permanently assigned to one district, the system creates procedural uniformity, eliminates the creation of "local rules", and attempts to prevent possible favoritism. This process is known as "riding the circuit."[21]

THE NORTH CAROLINA DISTRICT COURT DIVISION

The district court division of the General Court of Justice is comprised of all **district courts** in the state. The state is divided into forty district court districts, each with an assigned number of judges. The district court sits in the county seat of each county, as well as in other cities and towns that have been specifically authorized by the General Assembly.

District judges are elected by the voters of their district court district and must be a resident of that district. They serve terms of four years and must serve full-time. They are prohibited from practicing law during their terms of office.[22] In addition to district judges, district courts also have magistrates, who are officers of the district court. The General Assembly has established a minimum and maximum quota of magistrates for each county. Every county must have at least one magistrate. Magistrates serve two-year terms upon appointment by the senior superior court judge.[23] Currently, there are approximately 700 magistrates in North Carolina.[24] To be eligible to be nominated to serve as a magistrate, an individual must be a resident of the county for which s/he is appointed and must have either a four-year college degree or a two-year associate degree and four years of work experience in a related field.[25]

There are four main types or categories of district court jurisdiction: civil, criminal, juvenile, and magisterial. **Civil jurisdiction** is primarily concurrent between the superior and district trial divisions. The only exceptions are areas in which the superior court has exclusive original jurisdiction, including the probate of wills and the administration of estates. In general, district courts have jurisdiction over all civil cases involving $10,000 or less while the superior court hears cases that involve more than $10,000. However, while this convention is generally followed, it is not mandatory and there are times when cases are filed in the "wrong" division. In addition, some "small claims" civil cases may be heard by a magistrate.

Criminal jurisdiction is more clear-cut. Felony cases must be tried in superior court, so in these cases the district court can only conduct preliminary hearings. However, the district court has original jurisdiction over criminal cases involving misdemeanors and infractions. There are no criminal jury trials in district court.[26] Very minor criminal cases may be tried before a magistrate. **Juvenile cases** also fall under the jurisdiction of the district court. The district court hears cases that involve delinquents under the age of 16 or abused, neglected, undisciplined, or dependent children under the age of 18.

Finally, **magisterial jurisdiction** includes both criminal and civil cases, although it is clearly limited. Magistrates accept guilty pleas or pleas of responsibility for minor misdemeanors and traffic violations, accept waivers of trial and pleas of guilty to certain traffic, alcoholic beverage, littering, and other violations, and accept waivers of trial and pleas of guilty in worthless check cases involving checks of no more than $2,000. Magistrates also issue search and arrest warrants and set bail. They have the authority to try small claims cases involving sums of up to $4,000. These are always bench trials (trials without a jury) and frequently the parties involved are not represented by attorneys. These cases may be appealed from the magistrate's court to the district court where the appellant will receive a new trial. Magistrates are also the only civil officials in North Carolina authorized to perform a marriage ceremony.[27]

SPECIAL COURTS

North Carolina has a number of special or "innovative" courts that have been developed "to deal with certain problems where the traditional adversarial system is not always appropriate."[28] These include family courts, business courts, and drug treatment courts.

Family Courts were established in 1998. There are currently eight districts that operate family courts, covering a total of 16 counties. Family courts are unified courts that handle a variety of legal issues for individual families. These may include divorce, child abuse or neglect, child custody, visitation, termination of parental rights, adoptions, juvenile delinquency charges, domestic violence, involuntary commitments, and so on. The court attempts to help families solve their problems without going before a judge, by providing referrals to counselors, mediators, education programs, and other necessary services. If it is necessary for the family to go before a court for a hearing, family court assigns all issues to the same judge, rather than assigning each issue separately to a different judge. By having one judge handle all family matters, the judge is able to see the "big picture", better understand the needs of the specific family, and provide more consistent service to the family as a whole.

Family courts are administered by the chief district court judge, who is assisted by a family court administrator and a number of case managers (one for every two family court judges). Case managers are responsible for ensuring that all issues involving a specific family are assigned to the same judge, for ensuring that cases meet family court time standards for case disposal, and for coordinating family service programs.[29]

Business courts are operated through the superior court division. Cases are assigned to the business court by the Chief Justice of the Supreme Court, who assigns a special superior court judge to handle all pretrial and trial matters pertaining to that case. This allows the assigned judge to develop the necessary knowledge, understanding, and expertise relating to the legal issues involved in the case.[30]

Drug treatment courts focus on criminals whose activities relate to drug abuse. These courts will be discussed in more detail in Chapter 10.

COURT ADMINISTRATION

The Administrative Office of the Courts

The **Administrative Office of the Courts** (AOC) was established in 1965 and is responsible for the administration of the state judicial department. The director and assistant director of the AOC are appointed by the Chief Justice of the North Carolina Supreme Court.[31] One of the major responsibilities of the AOC is to prepare and administer the annual budget of the North Carolina court system. In 2002, the court system's budget was over $360 million.[32] In addition, the AOC is responsible for providing a wide variety of support services to the court system. These include:

- purchasing equipment and supplies
- providing personnel services
- preparing and distributing standardized records and forms
- compiling and distributing statistical data on the operation of the courts
- developing efficient computerized systems for record-keeping, data processing, and the provision of information
- developing training programs for court officials
- developing and publishing the rotation schedule for superior court judges

The AOC also administers several important programs within the North Carolina Judicial Department. The **Guardian Ad Litem Program** trains community volunteers to act as advocates for abused and neglected children, make recommendations to the court for those services needed by each child, and work to keep children safe and obtain permanent homes for them. The **Sentencing Services Program** is a network of state and county level programs that provide a wide variety of useful sentencing information to judges in criminal cases. According to NCGS §7A-773, the sentencing services program is responsible for:

(1) Identifying offenders who:

(1) Are charged with or have been offered a plea by the State for a felony offense for which the class of offense and prior record level authorize the court to impose an active punishment, but do not require that it do so;

(2) Have a high risk of committing future crimes without appropriate sanctions and interventions; and

(3) Would benefit from the preparation of an intensive and comprehensive sentencing plan of the type prepared by sentencing services programs.

(2) Preparing detailed sentencing services plans ... for presentation to the sentencing judge.

(3) Contracting or arranging with public or private agencies for services described in the sentencing plan.

The Judicial Standards Commission

The **Judicial Standards Commission** was created in 1973. The Commission is composed of seven members, including one Court of Appeals judge, on superior court judge, one district court judge, two members of the State Bar who have been actively practicing in North Carolina for at least 10 years, and two citizens, appointed by the governor, who are not judges or attorneys. Commission members serve terms of six years and may not be reappointed.[33]

The purpose of the Commission is to review and investigate complaints made by citizens against judges in the North Carolina Judicial Department and to make recommendations for the disposal of those complaints. This may include recommendations for censure or even removal of the judge in question. Complaints may relate to the qualifications of a judge or to the judge's conduct. Judges are entitled to a due process hearing after the complaint has been investigated by the Commission. The grounds for censure or removal of a judge are specifically outlined in NCGS §7A-376. They include:

- wilful misconduct in office
- wilful and persistent failure to perform judicial duties
- habitual intemperance
- conviction of any crime that involves moral terpitude
- conduct prejudicial to the administration of justice

The Commission may also recommend to the Supreme Court that a judge should be removed because of the development of a mental or physical incapacity that interferes with the performance of judicial duties, if that incapacity is, or is likely to become, permanent.

The State Judicial Council

The **State Judicial Council** was established by the General Assembly in 1999. It has a total of 18 members, including the Chief Justice of the North Carolina Supreme Court and the Chief Judge of the Court of appeals, as well as district attorneys, public defenders, superior and district court judges, clerks and magistrate, attorneys, and members of the general public who are not attorneys. All members serve terms of four years and may serve no more than two consecutive full terms.[34]

According to NCGS §7A-409.1(a), the duties of the Judicial Council include:

(1) Study the judicial system and report periodically to the Chief Justice on its findings;
(2) Advise the Chief Justice on priorities for funding;
(3) Review and advise the Chief Justice on the budget prepared by the Director of the Administrative Office of the Courts for submission to the General Assembly;
(4) Study and recommend to the General Assembly the salaries of justices and judges;
(5) Recommend to the General Assembly changes in the expense allowances, benefits, and other compensation for judicial officials;
(6) Recommend the creation of judgeships; and
(7) Advise or assist the Chief Justice, as requested, on any other matter concerning the operation of the courts.

In addition, the council is responsible for making recommendations on the development and revision of performance standards for all courts and all judicial personnel, studying and making recommendations on methods for evaluating courts and judicial personnel, studying and making recommendations on guidelines for cases assessment and management, monitoring the use of alternative dispute resolution by the courts, recommending changes in judicial district or division boundaries, and monitoring the administration of justice throughout the state.[35]

NORTH CAROLINA CRIMINAL COURT PROCEDURES

The basic procedures involved in a criminal trial, including the pretrial activities, are similar in most states. In North Carolina, the process begins when the police are notified (or in some other way discover) that a crime has been committed and they initiate an investigation into that crime. The procedures discussed in this section apply specifically to felony offenses; however, the procedures for misdemeanors are extremely similar.

Arrest and Booking

After the police have determined both that a crime has in fact been committed and that a specific person committed the crime, they may place that individual under **arrest**. In some situations, the police may have obtained a **warrant for arrest** from a judge. It includes a statement of the crime of which the suspect is accused as well as an order directing a law enforcement officer to take the person into custody and bring him or her before a judicial official to answer to the charges made against him or her. NCGS §15A-304(b) specifies when a warrant for arrest may be issued while NCGS §15A-305(b) lists the situations under which an order for arrest may be issued. However, in North Carolina, the majority of arrests are made by police officers acting without a warrant. NCGS §154A-401(b) outlines those situations in which it is lawful for an officer to make an arrest without a warrant.

After a suspect has been arrested and taken to the county jail, he/she undergoes the **booking** or **police processing** procedure, which involves entering into the police record various facts about the suspect. At this time, the suspect will be photographed and fingerprinted and may be placed in a police lineup. The suspect will be informed of the cause of the arrest, or the charges against him or her, will be advised of his or her rights to communicate with friends and with legal counsel, and will be given reasonable opportunity and time to do so.[36]

Initial Appearance

After a defendant is taken into custody by the police, he or she has the right to an **initial appearance**, before a magistrate. At this initial appearance, the magistrate will inform the defendant of the charges against him or her, his or her right to communicate with legal counsel and friends, and how he or she may secure bail. If the arrest was made without a warrant, the magistrate will determine whether or not there is probable cause to believe that a crime was committed and that the arrested individual committed the crime.[37]

The magistrate will also consider whether or not the defendant is entitled to any form of **pretrial release**, including **bail**. Although the U.S. Supreme Court stated in *Stack v. Boyle*[38] that the U.S. Constitution does not guarantee the right to bail, the North Carolina General Statutes do provide a substantive right to bail in many cases. However, not everyone has a right to bail. GA §15A-533(a) does state that

> A defendant charged with any crime, whether capital or noncapital, who is alleged to have committed this crime while still residing in or subsequent to his escape or during an unauthorized absence from involuntary commitment in a mental health facility designated or licensed by the Department of Health and Human Services, and whose commitment is determined to be still valid by the judge or judicial officer authorized to determine pretrial release to be valid, has no right to pretrial release...

When the magistrate or judge considers pretrial release of a defendant, s/he considers a variety of factors, including:

- the nature of the charge against the defendant

- the weight of the evidence against the defendant

- community ties that might prevent or deter the defendant from fleeing.

The magistrate has four main options when setting conditions of pretrial release. These include:

- releasing the defendant on his or her personal recognizance, with a written promise to appear (no bail required)
- requiring a payment of cash bail in exchange for pretrial release
- requiring a payment of non-cash bail (usually a property bond where the defendant deposits some form of property as collateral for release)
- releasing the defendant into the custody of an individual or agency that agrees to supervise the defendant.[39]

At this time, the defendant may be asked to make an initial **plea** to the charges. A defendant has three plea options: guilty, not guilty, or *nolo contendere* ("no contest"). A plea of no contest indicates that, while not admitting guilt, the defendant does not contest the charges. This plea may only be made with the consent of the judge and the prosecutor and is not always permitted.[40]

First Appearance before a District Court Judge

If the defendant is charged with a felony, he or she must be brought before a district court judge for a **first appearance**. In some cases, the initial appearance and first appearance may be consolidated by holding the initial appearance before a district court judge rather than a magistrate.[41] Unless the defendant has been granted pretrial release, the first appearance must take place within 96 hours of arrest, or at the first regular session of the district court, whichever comes first.[42] During the first appearance the judge must determine if the defendant has retained counsel or, if the defendant indigent and cannot afford to hire an attorney, had counsel assigned. If an indigent defendant has not had an attorney assigned, the judge will appoint one at this time.[43] In addition, during the first appearance, the judge will inform the defendant of the charges that have been placed against him or her and, if the defendant was not granted pretrial release at the initial appearance, review the defendant's eligibility for pretrial release.[44] The judge will also schedule a probable cause hearing or obtain a waiver of the hearing from the defendant.

Probable Cause Hearing

The next step is a **probable cause hearing**. This is scheduled by the district court judge during the first appearance. Unless the defendant waives his or her right to this hearing, or it is continued at the request of either the prosecution or defense, it must be scheduled no more than 15 working days after the first appearance before the district court judge, or the first day of the next session of the district court, whichever comes first. However, it may not be scheduled less than five days after the first appearance, unless both the prosecutor and the defendant consent.[45] The purpose of this hearing is to ensure that the state has enough evidence to proceed with the case against the defendant. Unless the judge finds probable cause that the defendant committed the crime of which s/he is charged, or some lesser included offense, the judge must dismiss the case.

The procedure for the probable cause hearing is outlined in NCGS §15A-611, which states that:

> (a) At the probable-cause hearing:
>   (1) A prosecutor must represent the State.
>   (2) The defendant may be represented by counsel.
>   (3) The defendant may testify as a witness in his own behalf and call and examine other witnesses, and produce other evidence in his behalf.
>   (4) Each witness must testify under oath or affirmation and is subject to cross-examination.
> (b) The State must by nonhearsay evidence, or by evidence that satisfies an exception to the hearsay rule, show that there is probable cause to believe that the offense charged has been committed and that there is probable cause to believe that the defendant committed it...

The judge at a probable cause hearing must take one of three actions:

1. If the judge finds that the defendant probably committed the crime, or a lesser included offense, and the offense is a felony, the judge must bind the defendant over to superior court. The judge must also bind the defendant over to superior court if the defendant waives probable cause in a felony charge.

2. If the judge finds no probable cause regarding the charged offense, but does find probable cause for a lesser offense that is under the jurisdiction of the district court, s/he may set the case for trial in district court.

3. If the judge finds no probable cause for any charge, the case must be dismissed.[46]

If the defendant is bound over for trial in either superior or district court, the judge also must again review the defendant's eligibility for pretrial release.[47]

Indictment, Information, and the Grand Jury

According to Article I, Section 22 of the North Carolina State Constitution,

> Except in misdemeanor cases initiated in the District Court Division, no person shall be put to answer any criminal charge but by indictment, presentment, or impeachment. But any person, when represented by counsel, may, under such regulations as the General Assembly shall prescribe, waive indictment in noncapital cases.

In other words, the State Constitution guarantees that no one may be placed on trial for a felony offense without his or her consent, unless indicted by a **grand jury**. This is an attempt to protect individuals against unfounded accusations and unjust prosecution. Thus, once a felony has been bound over to superior court by a district court judge, the defendant must be indicted, or formally accused in writing, by a grand jury.

Chapter 15A, Article 31 of the General Statutes outlines the procedures relating to the grand jury. The purpose of the grand jury is to determine whether or not there is sufficient evidence to justify a formal **indictment** against an accused individual. The grand jury is presented with a **bill of indictment**, a written accusation that charges a specific individual with the commission of one or more crimes. The bill also includes a list of witnesses that the grand jury will examine. The grand jury does not try the question of the defendant's guilt or innocence, but attempts to answer two key questions:

1. Is it probable that a crime was committed?

2. Is it probable that the defendant committed the crime?

After hearing all the witnesses listed on the bill, the grand jury deliberates and votes. If the grand jury decides that there is sufficient evidence to believe that a crime has been committed and that there is probable cause to believe that the defendant committed the crime, a **true bill of indictment** is issued and the defendant may then be tried. In North Carolina, the grand jury is composed of 12 to 18 individuals.[48] For a true bill to be issued, a minimum of 12 members of the grand jury must vote to return an indictment.[49] If the grand jury finds that there is insufficient evidence to show that the accused individual committed the crime, the bill of indictment is returned to the court as **not a true bill** and the case will be dismissed.

According to NCGS §15A-624(e), ""Grand jury proceedings are secret and, except as expressly provided ... members of the grand jury and all persons present during its sessions shall keep its secrets and refrain from disclosing anything which transpires during any of its sessions."

In a capital case, or in a case where the defendant is not represented by counsel, the indictment may not be waived.[50] However, in other cases, the prosecution may initiate felony charges in superior court without an indictment, by filing a **bill of information**, or written accusation, with the court. The bill of information charges the defendant with the commission of the specified crimes.

Plea Bargaining

While **plea bargaining** is not a formal stage of the criminal justice process, it is an extremely important process in every state, including North Carolina. The use of plea conferences in superior court is discussed in NCGS §15A-1021. The statute essentially allows the defense and the prosecution to discuss the possibility that, if the defendant pleads guilty or no contest to a crime, the prosecutor will reciprocate in some way. Possible actions by the prosecutor in exchange for a plea of guilty or no contest include:

- the prosecutor will not file charges against the defendant
- the prosecutor will dismiss charges against the defendant
- the prosecutor will move for the dismissal of additional charges against the defendant
- the prosecutor will recommend a specific sentence
- the prosecutor will not oppose a specific sentence requested by the defense[51]

According to the statute, the defendant's presence at the plea negotiations is not required if s/he is represented by counsel. The trial judge is allowed, but not required, to participate in the discussions. Plea bargaining may occur at any time in the pre-trial process but usually occurs prior to the indictment.

A superior court judge may not accept a plea of guilty or no contest from the defendant unless the judge first speaks directly to the defendant on the following topics:

- The judge must inform the defendant of his or her right to remain silent and that any statements made may be used against him or her

66

- The judge must ensure that the defendant understands the nature of the charge

- The judge must inform the defendant that s/he has the right to plead not guilty to the charge

- The judge must inform the defendant that by pleading guilty or no contest, s/he is waiving his or her rights to a jury trial and to be confronted by witnesses

- The judge must determine that the defendant is satisfied with his or her counsel (if the defendant is represented by counsel)

- The judge must inform the defendant of the maximum possible sentence on the charge to which s/he is being sentenced

- If the defendant is not a U.S. citizen, the judge must inform the defendant that a plea of guilty or no contest may result in deportation, exclusion of admission to the U.S., or denial of naturalization

Pre-Trial Motions

There are a number of **pre-trial motions** that may be filed in court. A **motion to dismiss** is filed by the defense and asks that the case against the defendant be dismissed. Possible grounds for dismissal include:

- the statute which the defendant is charged with violating is unconstitutional

- the statute of limitations has expired

- the defendant's right to a speedy trial was denied

- the defendant's constitutional rights were violated in such a way that irreparable damage was done to the defendant's case preparation

- the defendant has been tried on these charges (double jeopardy)

- the court does not have jurisdiction over the offense charged

- the defendant was granted immunity from prosecution[52]

A **motion to continue** requests that the case be delayed for a specific period of time. This may be filed by either the defense or the prosecution. A **motion for a change of venue** requests that the location of the trial be changed on the grounds that it is not possible to obtain a fair and impartial trial in the county where the case is currently pending because there is a significant prejudice against the defendant. In response to this motion, the judge has the option to transfer the case to another county or to order a special venire, which involves trying the case in front of a jury brought in from another county.[53]

A **motion to suppress evidence** considers whether evidence was obtained illegally and should therefore be prohibited for use as evidence in court. According to NCGS §15A-974, the grounds for suppressing evidence include:

(1) Its exclusion is required by the Constitution of the United States or the Constitution of the State of North Carolina; or
(2) It is obtained as a result of a substantial violation of the provisions of this Chapter. In determining whether a violation is substantial, the court must consider all the circumstances, including:
   a. The importance of the particular interest violated;
   b. The extent of the deviation from lawful conduct;
   c. The extent to which the violation was willful
   d. The extent to which exclusion will tend to deter future violations of this Chapter.

Trial

Less than ten percent of all felony and misdemeanor cases go to a formal criminal **trial**; the vast majority are disposed of by a plea of guilty on the part of the defendant. If the defendant enters a plea of not guilty and the case does go to trial, the procedure is the same regardless of whether the case involves a felony or a misdemeanor.

According to the Sixth Amendment to the U.S. Constitution, all defendants have the right to a speedy, public, and impartial trial. The North Carolina State Constitution also guarantees the right to a **jury trial** in all criminal cases.[54] In North Carolina, criminal cases are tried before a twelve-member jury and the verdict must be unanimous before the defendant may be found guilty of any charge.[55]

The basic steps involved in a superior court trial in North Carolina are outlined in Chapter 15A, Subchapter XII of the General Statutes.

Jury Selection

The first step in a trial is the **selection of the jury**. Each county in North Carolina has a three-member **jury commission** that is responsible for preparing a list of prospective jurors qualified to serve. This **venire**, or list of possible jurors, is compiled using the voter registration records of the county as well as the list of licensed drivers residing in the county.[56] According to NCGS §9-3, to be qualified to serve on a jury in North Carolina, an individual:

- must be a citizen of North Carolina and a resident of the county
- must not have served as a juror in the past two years
- must be at least 18 years of age
- must be physically and mentally competent
- must be able to hear and understand the English language

- must have not been convicted of a felony or have pleaded guilty or *nolo contendere* to an indictment charging a felony (or have had their citizenship restored)
- must not have been adjudged *non compos mentis*

The process of jury selection is known as **voir dire** and involves an examination of the prospective jurors by the court and by the attorneys for both the prosecution and the defense. The purpose of the *voir dire* is to determine whether each potential juror is impartial and will be able to render a fair verdict in a case. Potential jurors are placed under oath and then questioned by the judge, prosecutor, and defense counsel.

During the *voir dire* process, both the defense and the district attorneys are allowed to make challenges, or to object to the inclusion of certain potential trial jurors. North Carolina allows two types of challenges to prospective jurors. **Challenges for cause** generally are based on the attorney's belief that the juror is biased in some way that will prevent him or her from acting impartially and without prejudice during the trial. NCGS §15A-1212 outlines the specific grounds on which a challenge for cause may be made:

> A challenge for cause to an individual juror may be made by any party on the ground that the juror:
> (1) Does not have the qualifications required...
> (2) Is incapable by reason of mental or physical infirmity of rendering jury service.
> (3) Has been or is a party, a witness, a grand juror, a trial juror, or otherwise has participated in civil or criminal proceedings involving a transaction which relates to the charge against the defendant.
> (4) Has been or is a party adverse to the defendant in a civil action, or has complained against or been accused by him in a criminal prosecution.
> (5) Is related by blood or marriage within the sixth degree to the defendant or the victim of the crime.
> (6) Has formed or expressed an opinion as to the guilt or innocence of the defendant. It is improper for a party to elicit whether the opinion formed is favorable or adverse to the defendant.
> (7) Is presently charged with a felony.
> (8) As a matter of conscience, regardless of the facts and circumstances, would be unable to render a verdict with respect to the charge in accordance with the law of North Carolina.
> (9) For any other cause is unable to render a fair and impartial verdict.

Peremptory challenges may be used by either attorney to remove potential jurors from the jury panel without giving specific reasons. The number of peremptory challenges allowed is determined by statute. If the offense to which the defendant is charged is punishable by death or life imprisonment, each defendant is allowed 14 peremptory challenges and the state is allowed 14 peremptory challenges for each defendant. In noncapital cases, each party is entitled to six peremptory challenges.[57]

After the selection of the jury is completed, the jurors are impaneled and sworn in by the court. The process of impaneling the jury includes the following instructions given by the clerk of the court:

"Members of the jury, you have been sworn and are now impaneled to try the issue in the case of State of North Carolina versus _____. You will sit together, hear the evidence, and render your verdict accordingly."[58]

Opening Statements

Both the prosecutor and the defense attorney are entitled to make an opening statement which provides all the participants in the trial, especially the jury, with an overview of the facts of the case. In North Carolina, the prosecutor makes the first statement. After the prosecution's opening remarks are completed, the defense may make an opening statement immediately or may choose to wait until after the prosecutor has introduced the evidence in support of the charge.[59]

Presentation of the Prosecution's Evidence

After the opening statements are completed, the prosecution begins to present evidence in support of the charge that has been brought against the defendant. The prosecution presents first because the state is bringing the charge against the defendant and, because of the presumption of innocence, has assumed the burden of proof. The state is required by law to present evidence.[60] Evidence submitted into court may include documents, pictures, recordings, depositions, objects, pictures, or witness testimony. The judge determines the admissibility of each piece of evidence, based on the rules set forth in Chapter 8 of the General Statutes (Evidence). These rules are intended primarily to ensure that unreliable evidence, or evidence that was illegally obtained, is not accepted into court.

The prosecutor generally begins with **direct examination** of the prosecution's first witness, who is obviously expected to give evidence to support the state's case against the defendant. After the prosecutor finishes questioning the witness, the defense is allowed to **cross-examine** the same witness. If the prosecutor wishes, s/he may then return to ask the witness more questions in a process known as **re-direct examination**. Following this, the defense attorney has the option to question the witness once more during the **re-cross examination**. This procedure is repeated for each witness called by the prosecution.

Presentation of the Defense's Evidence

After the prosecution has presented all its evidence and called all its witnesses, the defense may then offer evidence. Unlike the state, the defense is not required by law to offer evidence at trial.[61] If the defense attorney chose not to make an opening statement at the start of the trial, s/he may make one prior to presenting evidence.

In many cases, the defense will begin by putting forth a motion for dismissal, on the grounds that the evidence offered by the prosecution was insufficient to sustain a conviction.[62] If the motion is denied, the defense presents its evidence.

The procedure for the presentation of the evidence by the defense is similar to that of the prosecution: direct examination, cross examination, re-direct, and re-cross. The defendant is not required to testify at any point in the trial; both the U.S. Constitution and the North Carolina State Constitution protect the defendant against self-incrimination.

Rebuttal and Surrebuttal

After the defense has presented its evidence, each side is given the opportunity to offer rebuttal evidence relating to the evidence presented by the opposing party. The judge may also allow the presentation of new evidence. In general, the prosecutor first presents a **rebuttal**, possibly including additional evidence that may nullify or challenge that presented by the defense, after which the defense is given the opportunity to present a **surrebuttal** case.[63]

Closing Arguments

Once all the evidence is presented, each side is given the opportunity to make a **closing argument** which is addressed directly to the jury.[64] During this stage of the trial, each attorney reviews and summarizes the evidence that best supports his or her side of case, discusses any inferences that may be drawn from that evidence, and points out weaknesses in the opponent's case.

Instructions to the Jury

After the final closing arguments are completed, the judge is required to provide instructions to the jury regarding any legal issues or points of law which are applicable to the case.[65] This step is also known as **charging the jury**. The judge may not express any opinions and is not required to review or summarize the evidence, nor to explain the application of the law to the evidence.[66]

Jury Deliberation and Verdict Rendition

After the judge has charged the jury, the jury retires to the jury room for **deliberation**.[67] At this time, the jurors discuss the case and attempt to come to agreement on a verdict concerning the guilt or innocence of the defendant. North Carolina law requires that all jurors agree on a guilty verdict before the defendant can be convicted of the charge.[68] If the jurors are unable to agree on a verdict after a reasonable period of time, they are **deadlocked** and considered to be a "**hung jury**." If this happens, the judge will declare a **mistrial** and the case may have to be retried in front of a new jury.

If the jurors come to an agreement on a **verdict**, they are returned to the courtroom and the verdict is read in open court. Either the defense or the prosecution is entitled to request a poll of the jury to ensure that each member of the jury agrees with the verdict and that no member was coerced or intimidated into agreeing, or agreed simply out of exhaustion. If any juror responds negatively, the court must refuse to accept the verdict and direct the jury to resume deliberations. The judge also has the right to require the jury to be polled.[69]

If the verdict of the jury is not guilty, the trial is over and the defendant must be immediately discharged from custody and is entitled to the return of any bail money and the exoneration of any sureties. The trial court judge is required to accept a verdict of not guilty. Because of the constitutional protections against double jeopardy, the defendant may never be tried in state court for those same charges.

Proceedings Between the Verdict and the Sentence

If the defendant is found guilty, he/she will be sentenced. However, after a verdict of guilty is rendered and before the sentencing phase of the trial, the defendant may make a **post-trial motion** to set aside or modify the verdict. If the judge sets aside the verdict, the defendant may be entitled to a dismissal, a reduction of the charges, or a new trial. These motions are rarely granted.

The Sentence

If the defendant is found guilty, s/he will be sentenced by a judge. In most cases, the trial judge will pronounce the **sentence**, although in some situations it may be necessary for sentence to be pronounced by a different judge. The sentencing process is discussed in more detail in Chapter 6.

Appeal

If the defendant is convicted of a crime, s/he may have the option of **appealing** the conviction to the Appellate Division of the General Court of Justice. In some cases, the prosecution may also have the right to appeal a verdict of not guilty, although this is a much less common occurrence. An appeal does not involve retrying a case or re-examining the factual issues surrounding the crime; it only involves an examination or review of the legal issues involved in the case. The purpose of an appeal is to make certain that the defendant received a fair trial and that he or she was not deprived of any constitutional rights at any time.

NOTES

1. North Carolina State Constitution, Article IV, §2
2. North Carolina State Constitution, Article IV, §5
3. Brannon, J.G. (2001). *The Judicial System in North Carolina.* Available online at (http://www.nccourts.org/Citizens/Publications/Documents/JudicialSystem.pdf)
4. See 28 U.S.C. 113
5. The Federal Judiciary home page (http://www.uscourts.gov/)
6. North Carolina State Constitution, Article IV, §6
7. North Carolina General Statutes, §7A-10(a)
8. North Carolina State Constitution, Article IV, §16
9. North Carolina State Constitution, Article IV, §22
10. North Carolina State Constitution, Article IV, §12 (1)
11. North Carolina General Statutes, §7A-26
12. North Carolina General Statutes, §7A-27(a)
13. North Carolina General Statutes, §7A-32
14. North Carolina State Constitution, Article IV, §7
15. North Carolina State Constitution, Article IV, §16
16. The North Carolina Court System home page: Court of Appeals of North Carolina (http://www.nccourts.org/Courts/Appellate/Appeal/Default.asp)
17. Brannon, J.G. (2001), *op. cit.*
18. See North Carolina General Statutes, §7A-41 for a list of superior court divisions and districts
19. North Carolina General Statutes, §7A-41.2
20. North Carolina State Constitution, Article IV, §9(1)
21. Brannon, J.G. (2001), *op. cit.*
22. North Carolina General Statutes, §7A-140
23. North Carolina General Statutes, §7A-171
24. Brannon, J.G. (2001), *op. cit.*
25. North Carolina General Statutes, §7A-171.2

26. North Carolina General Statutes, §7A-196(b)
27. North Carolina General Statutes, §7A-292(9)
28. Brannon, J.G. (2001), *op. cit.*, p.11.
29. The North Carolina Court System home page: Family Court
    (http://www.nccourts.org/Citizens/CPrograms/Family/Default.asp)
30. The North Carolina Business Court home page (http://www.ncbusinesscourt.net/)
31. North Carolina General Statutes, §7A-341 and §7A-342
32. The North Carolina Court System home page: AOC Court Administration
    (http://www.nccourts.org/Courts/CRS/AOCAdmin/)
33. North Carolina General Statutes, §7A-375
34. North Carolina General Statutes, §7A-409
35. North Carolina General Statutes, §7A-409.1(b) - §7A-409.1(f)
36. North Carolina General Statutes, §15A-501
37. North Carolina General Statutes, §15A-511
38. *Stack v. Boyle*, 342 U.S. 1 (1951)
39. North Carolina General Statutes, §15A-534(a)
40. North Carolina General Statutes, §15A-1011
41. North Carolina General Statutes, §15A-601(b)
42. North Carolina General Statutes, §15A-601(c)
43. North Carolina General Statutes, §15A-603
44. North Carolina General Statutes, §15A-605
45. North Carolina General Statutes, §15A-606
46. North Carolina General Statutes, §15A-612
47. North Carolina General Statutes, §15A-614
48. North Carolina General Statutes, §15A-621
49. North Carolina General Statutes, §15A-623(a)
50. North Carolina General Statutes, §15A-642(b)
51. North Carolina General Statutes, §15A-1021(a)
52. North Carolina General Statutes, §15A-954(a)
53. North Carolina General Statutes, §15A-957 and §15A-958
54. North Carolina State Constitution, Article I, §24
55. North Carolina General Statutes, §15A-1201
56. North Carolina General Statutes, §9-1 and 9-2
57. North Carolina General Statutes, §15A-1217
58. North Carolina General Statutes, §15A-1216
59. North Carolina General Statutes, §15A-1221(a)(4)
60. North Carolina General Statutes, §15A-1221(a)(5)
61. North Carolina General Statutes, §15A-1221(a)(6)
62. North Carolina General Statutes, §15A-1227
63. North Carolina General Statutes, §15A-1221(a)(7) and §15A-1226
64. North Carolina General Statutes, §15A-1221(a)(8)
65. North Carolina General Statutes, §15A-1221(a)(9)
66. North Carolina General Statutes, §15A-1232
67. North Carolina General Statutes, §15A-1221(a)(10)
68. North Carolina General Statutes, §15A-1235
69. North Carolina General Statutes, §15A-1238

CHAPTER 6

SENTENCING IN NORTH CAROLINA

INTRODUCTION

After a criminal defendant pleads guilty or is found guilty in court by a judge or jury, the judge must impose a **sentence** of punishment upon the offender. A sentence is a penalty imposed on a defendant for the crime of which the defendant has been adjudicated guilty or to which the defendant has pled guilty or no contest. NCGS §15A-1340.12 discusses the purposes of sentencing, stating that:

> The primary purposes of sentencing a person convicted of a crime are to impose a punishment commensurate with the injury the offense has caused, taking into account factors that may diminish or increase the offender's culpability; to protect the public by restraining offenders; to assist the offender toward rehabilitation and restoration to the community as a lawful citizen; and to provide a general deterrent to criminal behavior.

Clearly, there are multiple goals or objectives in sentencing and these may at times conflict with one another, so that an attempt to meet one objective may make it difficult, or even impossible to also meet another objective. When this occurs, the sentencing judge must make a decision based on the individual case at hand as to which objectives have the higher priority.

In every case in which a conviction has been entered, the court is required to pronounce sentence. If the defendant has been found guilty on multiple counts, the court must pronounce sentence on each count. In all cases, the judge determines the final sentence, although in those cases where the defendant has been convicted of a capital crime, the jury provides the sentencing judge with a recommendation as to the sentence to be imposed.

TYPES OF SENTENCES

A variety of sentences may be imposed upon convicted offenders in North Carolina. Sentences acceptable in the North Carolina courts include:

- community sanctions (e.g., fines, restitution, treatment, community service, basic probation)
- intermediate sanctions (e.g., boot camp, house arrest with electronic monitoring, shock incarceration, intensive probation, assignment to a day reporting center or residential program)
- active sanctions (incarceration in a jail or prison)
- death (capital punishment)

Combinations of these sentences are also allowed. For example, a judge may order both imprisonment and a fine, or place an offender on probation and order the offender to pay victim restitution. However, the judge has only a limited amount of discretion when imposing a sentence; s/he must follow the sentencing guidelines set out in the General Statutes.[1]

WHEN SENTENCING OCCURS

If a defendant enters a plea of guilty or no contest to a felony charge, there is no trial and the court proceeds directly to the sentencing phase. The judge will hold a sentencing hearing, unless the defendant waives this hearing, and will impose a sentence.[2]

If the defendant enters a plea of not guilty and is then found guilty in a criminal trial, the sentence will be imposed at a sentencing hearing which may be held immediately following the trial or scheduled for a later date. The judge may order the probation department to prepare a pre-sentencing report before holding a sentencing hearing. This report contains information about the offender's background and about the circumstances of the crime.[3]

In a capital case, there must be a separate sentencing proceeding to determine whether the penalty shall be death or life imprisonment. This proceeding is conducted by the trial judge before the trial jury.[4] Sentencing in capital cases will be discussed in more detail in Chapter 7.

CONCURRENT VERSUS CONSECUTIVE SENTENCES

If an offender is convicted of multiple offenses at the same time, the General Statutes do allow, but do not require, the court to consolidate the crimes for judgment and impose a single sentence for all crimes. If the court chooses to do this, the judgment would include a sentence based on the class of offense and prior record level of the most serious offense committed by the offender.[5] If the court does not choose to consolidate the crimes for judgment, sentences may run either concurrently or consecutively, although unless the court specifically states otherwise, all sentences of imprisonment will be assumed to run concurrently.[6] **Concurrent sentences** are served at the same time while **consecutive sentences** are served in succession, one after the other.

The decision to impose consecutive rather than concurrent sentences is an important one as it can significantly increase the overall length of the offender's sentence. In general, superior court judges tend to impose consecutive sentences in cases that involve multiple distinct offenses and/or victims, in cases where the offender was on probation at the time of the current offense, and in cases where the offender's prior record was particularly bad.

NORTH CAROLINA'S STRUCTURED SENTENCING LAWS

Introduction to Structured Sentencing in North Carolina

In 1990, the **NC Sentencing and Policy Advisory Commission** was created by the General Assembly. The purpose of the Commission was to review the state's criminal sentencing policies and procedures and make recommendations to the Assembly. In 1993, after reviewing the recommendations of the Commission, the Assembly adopted Chapter 15A, Article 81B of the General Statutes, the Structured Sentencing Law. **Structured sentencing** applies to all criminal offenses in the state (felony and misdemeanor), except for the crime of impaired driving (DWI), committed on or after October 1, 1994.[7]

Structured sentencing provides judges with specific sentencing options regarding the length and type of sentence that may be imposed, using a point system based on the severity of the crime and the prior record level of the offender. The new law eliminated parole and identified three basic types or categories of punishments. An **active punishment** is one that "requires an offender to serve a sentence of imprisonment and is not suspended."[8] An **intermediate punishment** is a sentence that requires that the offender be placed on probation and also includes at least one of the following conditions: special probation, intensive probation assignment to a residential program or day-reporting center, or house arrest with electronic monitoring.[9] Finally, a **community punishment** is any punishment that does not include active or intermediate punishment, or probation.[10] Examples of community punishments include restitution, fines, treatment, and community service.

The law classifies felonies into ten levels of severity, ranging from Offense Class A through Offense Class I (Class B is divided into B1 and B2), based on the actual or potential harm to the victim of the crime. Violent crimes (those involving injury or the risk of injury to the victim) are considered to be more serious than property crimes. Prior records for felony offenders are divided into six levels based on the extent and seriousness of the offender's prior criminal history. Offenders with extensive prior records and/or prior records that include violent crimes are placed in the highest levels. Misdemeanor offenses are divided into four classes of severity and there are three levels of prior convictions.

Judges have a limited amount of discretion in the imposition of sentences. If a felony offender is convicted of a crime in a high offense category, or has high prior record levels, the judge must impose an active punishment. If the felony offender committed a crime in a low offense category or has low prior record levels, the judge must impose intermediate or community sanctions. For offenders who fall in the middle of the range, the judge has the option of choosing either an intermediate or an active punishment. In addition, the length of the sentence may be affected by aggravating or mitigating circumstances that are also specified in the statutes.

Factors Considered in Sentencing Felony Offenders

When a judge is sentencing an offender for a specific criminal offense, s/he considers two main factors: the severity of the offense (Class A through I) and the prior record level of the offender (Level I through VI). In addition, the judge may consider aggravating and mitigating factors.

The **severity of the offense** is specified in the conviction offense for which the sentence is being imposed. If the offender is being sentenced for a felony for which there is no specified classification, it is automatically considered to be a Class I felony (the lowest level).[11] The statutes also specify enhanced punishments for certain felony classes when specified conditions occur. For example, if a defendant is convicted of a Class A, B1, B2, C, D, or E felony and the defendant used, displaced, or threatened to use or display a firearm during the commission of that felony, the minimum term of imprisonment may be increased.[12] Similarly, under certain conditions, an offender convicted of a second or subsequent Class B1 felony may be sentenced to life imprisonment without parole.[13]

The second factor considered by the judge is the **prior record level** of the offender, if any. This assigns points for each prior conviction, based on the seriousness of the prior conviction, as follows:

- 10 points for each prior felony Class A conviction
- 9 points for each prior felony Class B1 conviction
- 6 points for each prior felony Class B2, C, or D conviction
- 4 points for each prior felony Class E, F, or G conviction
- 2 points for each prior felony Class H or I conviction
- 1 point for each prior misdemeanor conviction
- 1 point if all elements of the present offense are included in any prior offense for which the offender was convicted
- 1 point if the offense was committed while the offender was on supervised or unsupervised probation, parole, or post-release supervision, while incarcerated, or while escaping from a correctional institution.[14]

The points are then totaled and the prior record level is determined as follows:

- Level I - 0 points
- Level II - 1-4 points
- Level III - 5-8 points
- Level IV - 9-14 points
- Level V - 15-18 points
- Level VI - at least 19 points[15]

The judge may also consider evidence of aggravating and mitigating factors, if any, that are present in the offense and that may make an aggravated or mitigated sentence appropriate. However, the judge is not required to depart from the sentencing ranges defined in the statutes; NCGS §15A-1340.16(a) states that "...the decision to depart from the presumptive range is in the discretion of the court." **Aggravating factors** are circumstances about the crime or the offender which increase the seriousness of the crime or make it worse than usual in some way whereas **mitigating factors** make the crime less serious in some way. Aggravating factors that may affect the sentence are listed in NCGS §15A-1340.16(d):

(1)	The defendant induced others to participate in the commission of the offense or occupied a position of leadership or dominance of other participants.

(2)	The defendant joined with more than one other person in committing the offense and was not charged with committing a conspiracy.

(2a)	The offense was committed for the benefit of, or at the direction of, any criminal street gang, with the specific intent to promote, further, or assist in any criminal conduct by gang members, and the defendant was not charged with committing a conspiracy...

(3)	The offense was committed for the purpose of avoiding or preventing a lawful arrest or effecting an escape from custody.

(4)	The defendant was hired or paid to commit the offense.

(5)	The offense was committed to disrupt or hinder the lawful exercise of any governmental function or the enforcement of laws.

(6)	The offense was committed against or proximately caused serious injury to a present or former law enforcement officer, employee of the Department of Correction, jailer, fireman, emergency medical technician, ambulance attendant, justice or judge, clerk or assistant or deputy clerk of court, magistrate, prosecutor, juror, or witness against the defendant, while engaged in the performance of that person's official duties or because of the exercise of that person's official duties.

(7)	The offense was especially heinous, atrocious, or cruel.

(8)	The defendant knowingly created a great risk of death to more than one person by means of a weapon or device which would normally be hazardous to the lives of more than one person.

(9)	The defendant held public office at the time of the offense and the offense related to the conduct of the office.

(10)	The defendant was armed with or used a deadly weapon at the time of the crime.

(11)	The victim was very young, or very old, or mentally or physically infirm, or handicapped.

(12)	The defendant committed the offense while on pretrial release on another charge.

(13)	The defendant involved a person under the age of 16 in the commission of the crime.

(14)	The offense involved an attempted or actual taking of property of great monetary value or damage causing great monetary loss, or the offense involved an unusually large quantity of contraband.

(15)	The defendant took advantage of a position of trust or confidence to commit the offense.

(16)	The offense involved the sale or delivery of a controlled substance to a minor.

(17)	The offense for which the defendant stands convicted was committed against a victim because of the victim's race, color, religion, nationality, or country of origin.

(18)	The defendant does not support the defendant's family.

(18a)	The defendant has previously been adjudicated delinquent for an offense that would be a Class A, B1, B2, C, D, or E felony if committed by an adult.

(19)	The serious injury inflicted upon the victim is permanent and debilitating.

(20)   Any other aggravating factor reasonably related to the purposes of sentencing.

The statute also states that evidence that is necessary to prove an element of the offense for which the offender is being sentenced may not be used to prove any aggravating factor. The rationale behind this is that these facts have already been used against the offender in the determination of his or her guilt and may not be used a second time to enhance the sentence length. In addition, the statute prohibits any one item of evidence from being used to prove more than one aggravating factor.[16]

Mitigating factors that may be considered by the court and that may affect the sentence are listed in NCGS §15A-1340.16(e):

(1)   The defendant committed the offense under duress, coercion, threat, or compulsion that was insufficient to constitute a defense but significantly reduced the defendant's culpability.

(2)   The defendant was a passive participant or played a minor role in the commission of the offense.

(3)   The defendant was suffering from a mental or physical condition that was insufficient to constitute a defense but significantly reduced the defendant's culpability for the offense.

(4)   The defendant's age, immaturity, or limited mental capacity at the time of commission of the offense significantly reduced the defendant's culpability for the offense.

(5)   The defendant has made substantial or full restitution to the victim.

(6)   The victim was more than 16 years of age and was a voluntary participant in the defendant's conduct or consented to it.

(7)   The defendant aided in the apprehension of another felon or testified truthfully on behalf of the prosecution in another prosecution of a felony.

(8)   The defendant acted under strong provocation, or the relationship between the defendant and the victim was otherwise extenuating.

(9)   The defendant could not reasonably foresee that the defendant's conduct would cause or threaten serious bodily harm or fear, or the defendant exercised caution to avoid such consequences.

(10)   The defendant reasonably believed that the defendant's conduct was legal.

(11)   Prior to arrest or at an early stage of the criminal process, the defendant voluntarily acknowledged wrongdoing in connection with the offense to a law enforcement officer.

(12)   The defendant has been a person of good character or has had a good reputation in the community in which the defendant lives.

(13)   The defendant is a minor and has reliable supervision available.

(14)   The defendant has been honorably discharged from the United States armed services.

(15)   The defendant has accepted responsibility for the defendant's criminal conduct.

(16)   The defendant has entered and is currently involved in or has successfully completed a drug treatment program or an alcohol treatment program subsequent to arrest and prior to trial.

(17)   The defendant supports the defendant's family.

(18)   The defendant has a support system in the community.
(19)   The defendant has a positive employment history or is gainfully employed.
(20)   The defendant has a good treatment prognosis, and a workable treatment plan is available.
(21)   Any other mitigating factor reasonably related to the purposes of sentences.

The state bears the burden of proof to show, by a preponderance of evidence, that an aggravating factor exists, while the defense has the burden of proof to show that a mitigating factor exists. While the judge has the discretion to depart from the presumptive sentencing range based on the existence of these factors, if s/he does sentence the defendant to a term in the aggravated or mitigated range, s/he must provide a written explanation for this departure from the presumptive range.

Determining the Level of Punishment for Felony Offenders

NCGS §15A-1340.17 includes a chart that specifies the minimum authorized punishments for felony offenders, based on the felony class (rows) and the prior record level (columns). Each cell of the chart includes several key items of information:

- the sentence disposition (community, intermediate, or active punishment)[17]
- a presumptive range of minimum durations, expressed in months, if the sentence of imprisonment is not affected by aggravated or mitigated factors
- a presumptive range of minimum durations, expressed in months, if the court finds a mitigated sentence of imprisonment is justified
- a presumptive range of minimum durations, expressed in months, if the court finds an aggravated sentence of imprisonment is justified

Thus, for example, an offender who commits a Class C felony and has a prior record of Level II (1-4 points), would be given an active sentence of at least 80-100 months if there are no aggravating or mitigating factors. If aggravating factors were proven, the minimum sentence duration would increase to 100-125 months. If mitigating factors were proven, the minimum sentence duration would decrease to 60-80 months.

Once the minimum sentence is selected by the judge from the appropriate sentence range, the maximum sentence is automatically set by statute.[18] Basically, for Class F through Class I felonies, the maximum sentence length is 120 percent of the minimum sentence (rounded up to the next month). Maximum sentences lengths for Class B1 through Class E felonies are 120 percent of the minimum sentence (rounded up to the next month) plus an additional nine months for post-release supervision. While the structured sentencing law does allow for **earned time** for good behavior, work performed, or participation in rehabilitation, training, or educational programs, earned time only reduces the maximum sentence. The minimum sentence can never be reduced. Thus, if an offender was given a minimum active sentence of 100 months, the maximum sentence duration would be 129 months. The offender could earn up to 29 months off the sentence but would serve no less than 100 months regardless of good behavior or other factors.

While the structured sentencing laws provide mandatory sentencing guidelines, the judge still has a considerable amount of discretion within those guidelines. In almost one-third of the cells in the felony punishment chart, the judge has a choice of the type of sentence to impose (e.g., active vs intermediate). In addition, in every cell the judge must select a specific sentence length from within the range provided, and must decide whether to select that sentence from the aggravated, mitigated, or presumptive range. Factors which are commonly emphasized in selecting the specific length of sentence include not only the nature of the crime and the defendant's criminal history, but also the types of prior offenses, the time since the last offense, the offender's prison or probation history, and the defendant's status at the time of the current offense. Judges also consider individual characteristics such as the age, gender, family structure, employment status and history, level of remorse, and victim statements, as well as what is in the best interests of the community and public safety.

Sentencing Misdemeanor Offenders

The process for determining the sentence for an offender convicted of a misdemeanor is similar to that used for felony offenders. The offense severity level is specified in the offense for which the sentence is being imposed. There are four misdemeanor offense classes: A1, 1, 2, and 3. The prior conviction level is obtained by calculating the number of prior convictions the offender has. There are three prior conviction levels:

- Level I - 0 prior convictions
- Level II - 1-4 prior convictions
- Level III - at least 5 prior convictions[19]

NCGS §15A-1340.23 includes a chart that outlines the minimum and maximum sentences based on these factors. Using this chart, an offender who was convicted of a Class 1 misdemeanor and has 2 prior convictions would receive a sentence of 1-45 days. The judge has the option of giving the offender a community, intermediate, or active sentence of this duration. Any sentence within the specified limits is allowed.

Misdemeanor offenders who receive a sentence of imprisonment may also be sentenced to a fine. Maximum fines are specified by statute.[20]

VICTIM RIGHTS AND SERVICES

The Rights of Victims of Crime

The North Carolina State Constitution provides a "Victim's Bill of Rights" which lists a number of basic rights to which all victims of crimes in North Carolina are entitled. These rights include:

(a) The right as prescribed by law to be informed of and to be present at court proceedings of the accused.
(b) The right to be heard at sentencing of the accused in a manner prescribed by law, and at other times as prescribed by law or deemed appropriate by the court.
(c) The right as prescribed by law to receive restitution.

(d) The right as prescribed by law to be given information about the crime, how the criminal justice system works, the rights of victims, and the availability of services for victims.

(e) The right as prescribed by law to receive information about the conviction or final disposition and sentence of the accused.

(f) The right as prescribed by law to receive notification of escape, release, proposed parole or pardon of the accused, or notice of a reprieve or commutation of the accused's sentence.

(g) The right as prescribed by law to present their views and concerns to the Governor or agency considering any action that could result in the release of the accused, prior to such action becoming effective.

(h) The right as prescribed by law to confer with the prosecution.[21]

Victim Impact Statements

Victim impact statements are written reports or verbal statements that are given to the sentencing judge or jury for consideration when sentencing the defendant. Such a statement includes admissible evidence concerning the impact or effects of the crime upon the victim. As noted above, one of the basic rights of all crime victims, as stated in the North Carolina State Constitution, is the right to be heard at the sentencing of the accused offender. In addition, NCGS §15A-825 states that the criminal justice system must make reasonable effort to ensure that each victim of crime "has a victim impact statement prepared for consideration by the court." If the crime victim has died, the victim's next of kin is entitled to the rights of the victim, including the right to have a victim impact statement heard by the sentencing court.[22]

The evidence included in a victim impact statement may include a variety of items, including:

(1) A description of the nature and extent of any physical, psychological, or emotional injury suffered by the victim as a result of the offense committed by the defendant.

(2) An explanation of any economic or property loss suffered by the victim as a result of the offense committed by the defendant.

(3) A request for restitution and an indication of whether the victim has applied for or received compensation under the Crime Victims Compensation Act.[23]

While all victims have the right to a victim impact statement, no victim is required to present such a statement. The victim's choice not to present a statement may not affect the decisions made at the sentencing hearing. By statute, the court or jury may not draw any inferences or conclusions from a victim's decision not to offer impact evidence.[24]

The Right to Restitution

According to both the North Carolina State Constitution and the North Carolina General Statutes, all crime victims have the right to receive **restitution**.[25] During the sentencing hearing, the court is required to consider the imposition of restitution to the victim (or the victim's estate) as an element of the sentence.[26] This generally involves requiring the offender to pay a sum of money to the victim as reimbursement for injuries or damages due directly to the crime. In some cases, restitution may also be in a nonmonetary form (e.g., service to the community or to the victim).

When determining the amount of restitution to be imposed, the court considers a number of factors. These are discussed in NCGS §15A-1340.35. If the crime resulted in bodily injury to the victim, the court must consider the following factors:

- lost income resulting from the crime
- the cost of any medical or other related professional services, equipment, or devices that relate to physical, psychological, or psychiatric care that the victim required
- the cost of any necessary rehabilitation, physical therapy, or occupational therapy that the victim required
- the victim's funeral expenses and related services, if the crime resulted in the death of the victim

If the crime resulted in the damage, loss or destruction of the victim's property, the court must consider the return of the property to the owner. If it is not possible or practical to return the property, or if return would be inadequate, the court must consider either the value of the property at the time it was lost or damaged or the value of the property on the date of sentencing (minus the value of whatever part of the property was returned)

Other factors considered by the court relate to the defendant's possible ability to pay restitution. Obviously, it is meaningless for the court to order the defendant to pay restitution to the victim if the defendant does not have or is unable to earn the money required. These are discussed in NCGS §15-1340.36 and include:

- the defendant's resources (including real and personal property and the income derived from that property)
- the defendant's ability to earn
- the defendant's obligation to support any dependants
- any other matters that may affect the defendant's ability to make restitution

According to the General Statutes, court-ordered restitution does not prevent the victim from bringing a civil lawsuit against the defendant for damages resulting from the crime. However, if the victim wins a civil judgment, any restitution paid by the defendant will be credited against the judgment.[27]

The Right to Compensation

In addition to restitution, innocent victims of crimes committed in North Carolina may be eligible for **victim compensation**. While restitution is paid to the victim by the convicted offender, restitution is paid to the victim by the state. Victim compensation is discussed in the **North Carolina Crime Victims Compensation Act**, which is found in Chapter 15B of the General Statutes. In this Act, the General Assembly established the **North Carolina Crime Victims Compensation Commission** and gave it the authority to award (or deny) claims for compensation and reimbursement. The Commission has a total of seven members who serve terms of four years.[28] The Act assists crime victims who are attempting to obtain financial assistance for economic losses related to a violent crime. These losses may include lost wages, medical expenses, and replacement services such as child care expenses. Losses must be a direct result of the crime injury. Not all crimes are eligible for compensation. In North Carolina, awards of compensation are only given for economic losses and are only awarded for criminally injurious conduct (e.g., violent crimes).[29] Thus, an eligible victim is "a person who suffers personal injury or death proximately caused by criminally injurious conduct."[30]

All expenses must have been incurred as a direct result of a crime and no other source of reimbursement may be available. The victim compensation program is designed to be a victim's "last resort." All bills must first be filed with insurance companies before applying for compensation. Thus, for example, if the victim has adequate health insurance, s/he may not request compensation for medical expenses that are covered by that insurance. In addition, if the victim receives restitution from the offender to cover certain losses (e.g., lost income due to injury as a result of the crime), the victim may not also receive victim compensation for the same financial losses.

NCGS §15B-2(2) provides a list of claimants who are eligible to apply for and claim an award of compensation under the Act. They include:

(a) A victim;
(b) A dependent of a deceased victim;
(c) A third person who is not a collateral source and who provided benefit to the victim or his family other than in the course or scope of his employment, business, or profession;
(d) A person who is authorized to act on behalf of a victim, a dependent, or a third person described in subdivision c.

The statute also specifies that the claimant may not be the offender who committed the crime against the victim, nor may s/he be an accomplice of the offender.

Not everyone is eligible to claim victim compensation. According to the Crime Victims Compensation Commission, individuals who are not eligible include:

- a claimant who has insurance that pays the maximum amount authorized by the Act
- a claimant who does not incur any economic loss as a result of the crime within a period of one year after the crime (victims under the age of 10 at the time of injury may be compensated for economic loss occurring up to two years after the crime)
- a claimant who fails to file for compensation within one year from the date the crime occurred
- a claimant who does not report the crime to a law enforcement agency within 72 hours after the crime occurred
- a claimant who contributes to the criminal conduct
- a claimant who is the offender or an accomplice of the offender
- a claimant who fails to cooperate with the Commission

- a claimant whose award would benefit the offender or accomplice (unless the interests of justice require the award)
- a claimant who was confined in a correctional facility when the criminal event occurred
- a claimant who was committing a crime at the time the crime occurred[31]

For an award of compensation to be considered, it must be shown that

- a crime was committed
- the crime resulted in physical injury or death to a victim
- the crime was reported to a law enforcement agency within 72 hours
- the victim cooperated with law enforcement officials and the Victims Compensation Commission staff
- the victim was not committing any crime at the time of the incident[32]

There are limits to the amount of compensation that may be awarded. Currently, the maximum award in North Carolina is $30,000. However, if the victim dies as a result of the crime, an additional award of up to $3,500 may be paid to the victim's survivors for funeral expenses.[33]

NOTES

1. North Carolina General Statutes, Chapter 15A, Article 81B
2. North Carolina General Statutes, §15A-1334
3. North Carolina General Statutes, §15A-1332
4. North Carolina General Statutes, §15A-2000
5. North Carolina General Statutes, §15A-1340.15(b)
6. North Carolina General Statutes, §15A-1340.15(a) and §15A-1354(a)
7. North Carolina General Statutes, §15A-1340.10
8. North Carolina General Statutes, §15A-1340.11(1)
9. North Carolina General Statutes, §15A-1340.11(6)
10. North Carolina General Statutes, §15A-1340.11(2)
11. North Carolina General Statutes, §15A-1340.17(a)
12. North Carolina General Statutes, §15A-1340.16A
13. North Carolina General Statutes, §15A-1340.16B
14. North Carolina General Statutes, §15A-1340.14(b)
15. North Carolina General Statutes, §15A-1340.14(c)
16. North Carolina General Statutes, §15A-1340.16(d)
17. For the first row of the chart (Felony Class A), the prior record level is irrelevant - all such felonies are punishable by life imprisonment without parole or death as established by statute
18. North Carolina General Statutes, §15A-1340.17(e)
19. North Carolina General Statutes, §15A-1340.21
20. North Carolina General Statutes, §15A-1340.23(b)
21. North Carolina State Constitution, Article I, Section 37(1)
22. North Carolina General Statutes, §15A-830(b)
23. North Carolina General Statutes, §15A-833(a)

24.   North Carolina General Statutes, §15A-833(b)
25.   North Carolina State Constitution, Article I, Section 37(1)(c) and North Carolina General Statutes §15A-834
26.   North Carolina General Statutes, §15A-1340.34
27.   North Carolina General Statutes, §15A-1340.37
28.   North Carolina General Statutes, §15B-3
29.   North Carolina General Statutes, §15B-4
30.   North Carolina General Statutes, §15B-2(13)
31.   North Carolina Victims Compensation Services Division - Crime Victims Compensation Program home page (http://www.nccrimecontrol.org/vjs/cvcp0.htm)
32.   *Ibid*
33.   *Ibid*

CHAPTER 7

CAPITAL PUNISHMENT IN
NORTH CAROLINA

A HISTORY OF CAPITAL PUNISHMENT IN NORTH CAROLINA

North Carolina has had the death penalty since the colonial period. During this time, when North Carolina was an English colony, capital punishment was administered by both English common law and by legislation enacted by the state's Colonial Assembly. Executions were carried out at the local level during the colonial period and during the 19th century as well.

In 1910, the state took over the administration of capital punishment. The first offender to die in the North Carolina electric chair was Walter Morrison, who was executed on March 18, 1910. Morrison, a black male from Robison County, was convicted of the crime of rape. Between 1910 and 1961, a total of 362 people were executed in North Carolina.[1]

In 1972, the U.S. Supreme Court case of *Furman v. Georgia*[2] challenged the constitutionality of capital punishment in the United States. The Court ruled that the death penalty constituted "cruel and unusual punishment" and therefore was a violation of the Eighth Amendment of the U.S. Constitution, when juries were allowed uncontrolled discretion in imposing a sentence of death. The cases struck down death penalty laws throughout the country. A number of states, including North Carolina, responded to the *Furman* decision by removing all discretion and providing for mandatory sentences of death upon conviction for specified crimes. As a result, the number of offenders on death row in North Carolina increased to 120, a high for the state and, at the time, for the country as a whole.

In 1976, the U.S. Supreme Court responded to this in the case of *Woodson v. North Carolina*[3], in which it declared a mandatory sentence of death to be unconstitutional. The court ruled in *Woodson* that to prevent the death penalty from being a violation of the Eighth Amendment, it is necessary to have increased reliability in death cases, which requires that each defendant be evaluated individually to determine whether or not death is an appropriate punishment for the particular defendant and his or her specific crime. As a result of *Woodson*, all 120 inmates on death row had their sentences vacated. Many were retried and most received new sentences of life in prison. Between 1962 and 1983 there were no executions held in North Carolina.[4]

The North Carolina State Constitution addresses the issue of capital punishment in Article XI, Section 2, stating that:

> The object of punishments being not only to satisfy justice, but also to reform the offender and thus prevent crime, murder, arson, burglary, and rape, and these only, may be punishable with death, if the General Assembly shall so enact.

However, currently the only capital crime in North Carolina is that of first degree murder. This includes the crime of felony murder.

Since 1910, North Carolina has employed three different methods of execution: the electric chair, lethal gas, and lethal injection. The **electric chair** was the sole method of execution used between 1910 and 1936. However, on January 24, 1936, Allen Foster became the first inmate executed in the gas chamber. Two years later, on July 1, 1938, Wiley Brice became the last inmate to be executed in the electric chair. Between 1938 and 1983, the only method of execution used in the state was **lethal gas**. In 1983, the General Assembly passed legislation giving condemned offenders the right to choose death by **lethal injection**, rather than by lethal gas, if they so desired. Between 1984 and 1998, only two of the ten offenders executed in North Carolina chose death by lethal gas. In 1998, the General Assembly revised NCGS §15-187, abolishing abolished the use of lethal gas as a method of execution and requiring that all offenders sentenced to death by executed by lethal injection. Lethal injection is currently the only legal method of execution in North Carolina.[5]

On April 30, 2003, the North Carolina Senate passed Senate Bill S972, calling for a two-year moratorium on executions in North Carolina. The moratorium, which was approved by a vote of 29-21, is designed to allow the state to examine the fairness of the death penalty system. A moratorium does not remove any inmates from death row, unless the inmate needs a new trial or is found to be innocent during the period of the moratorium. It will, however, prevent any executions from being carried out during that time. Before the moratorium can be implemented, however, the measure must pass the North Carolina House of Representatives as well.

NORTH CAROLINA'S DEATH ROW

As of May 7, 2003, there were a total of 201 offenders on death row in North Carolina. Of these 196 are males. This number includes 69 white males, 115 black males, 7 Indian males, and 5 males of other races. There are 5 females on death row; 3 are white, 1 is black, and 1 is Indian. Norris C. Taylor, a black male from New Hanover County, is the longest resident; he has been on death row since 1979. Between 1976 and 2002, a total of 23 inmates were executed in North Carolina. Two of these were executed in 2002.[6]

North Carolina has a minimum age of 17 for the imposition of the death penalty; any individual who commits the crime of first degree murder while under the age of 17 will receive a sentence of life imprisonment without the possibility of parole. The only exception to this is an individual under the age of 17 who commits first degree murder while serving a sentence of incarceration for a prior conviction of murder or while on escape from a prison sentence that was imposed for a prior murder conviction.[7] The state also prohibits the use of capital punishment if the offender is mentally retarded.[8]

Male death row inmates are housed in the maximum security building at Central Prison in Raleigh, North Carolina. Each death row cellblock has two wings, each of which has two tiers holding a total of 16 single cells opening onto a dayroom area. Each individual cell contains a bed, toilet facilities, and a writing table mounted to the wall. Showers are located in the dayroom area, along with a television and a number of tables. Inmates are confined to their cellblock and required to stay in their cells between 11:00 pm and 7:00am. During other hours they may go into the dayroom and watch television. They do not receive work assignments. They are given a minimum of one hour per day for exercise and showers. They are escorted by correctional officers to dining halls by cellblock for each meal and to outdoor exercise areas two days a week. Inmates who violate regulations are placed in a segregation cellblock, are separated from other death row inmates during the daily exercise and shower period, and are required to eat all meals in their cells. Death row inmates are allowed only one visit per week, and a maximum of two visitors per visit. They are not allowed any physical contact with visitors. Christian and Islamic worship services, and a Bible study class, are held weekly.[9]

Female death row inmates are housed in the maximum security building at the North Carolina Correctional Institute for Women in Raleigh, North Carolina. There are a total of seven single cells, each of which contains a bed and toilet facilities. They also have a dayroom with a table, chairs, and a televison. All meals are eaten in the dayroom, and visits are held here as well. The women are given a minimum of one hour each day for showers and exercises. Conditions on the women's death row are similar to those of the men, although worship services are held only once a week.[10]

Between three and seven days prior to an inmate's date of execution, s/he is moved from death row to the death watch area in Central Prison. This area is located next to the execution chamber and contains a total of four cells, each of which has a bed, toilet facilities, and a writing table mounted to the wall. All the inmates personal belongings are moved to the death watch cell. There is a dayroom outside the cells but the inmates is only allowed out of the cell for a shower once a day, for a total of 15 minutes. However, a correctional officer and a sergeant are stationed in the dayroom around the clock whenever an inmate is in a death watch cell. Inmates on death watch are not allowed any contact with other inmates in the prison, although they may receive visits from family, attorneys, chaplains, psychologists, and any other individual authorized by the Division of Prisons. The inmate will remain in this area until taken to the execution chamber or until s/he receives a stay of execution.[11]

IMPOSING A SENTENCE OF DEATH IN NORTH CAROLINA

Like many states, North Carolina uses a bifurcated sentencing procedure, so that the determination of guilt or innocence and the sentencing decision occur at separate proceedings. According to NCGS §15A-2000(a), for a sentence of death to be imposed, several conditions must be met. The offender must first be convicted or adjudicated guilty of a capital felony, a crime which may be punishable by death. In addition, the state must have given notice of its intent to seek the death penalty for the crime. This notice must be given to the defendant and filed with the court on or before the date of the pretrial conference or the arraignment, whichever is later.[12] If the state does not give notice prior to trial of its intent to seek the death penalty, the court must, if the defendant is found guilty of first degree murder, impose a sentence of life imprisonment.[13]

The sentencing proceeding is held before the trial judge and the trial jury as soon as possible after the guilty verdict is returned by the jury. Both the prosecutor and the defense are allowed to present arguments for or against a sentence of death. The defense has the right to present the final argument.[14] The jury must consider both aggravating and mitigating circumstances before making a sentence recommendation. The only aggravating circumstances that may be considered by the jury are listed in NCGS §15A-2000(e):

(1) The capital felony was committed by a person lawfully incarcerated.

(2) The defendant had been previously convicted of another capital felony or had been previously adjudicated delinquent in a juvenile proceeding for committing an offense that would be a capital felony if committed by an adult.

(3) The defendant had been previously convicted of a felony involving the use or threat of violence to the person or had been previously adjudicated delinquent in a juvenile proceeding for committing an offense that would be a Class A, B1, B2, C, D, or E felony involving the use or threat of violence to the person if the offense had been committed by an adult.

(4) The capital felony was committed for the purpose of avoiding or preventing a lawful arrest or effecting an escape from custody.

(5) The capital felony was committed while the defendant was engaged, or was an aider or abettor, in the commission of, or an attempt to commit, or flight after committing or attempting to commit, any homicide, robbery, rape or a sex offense, arson, burglary, kidnapping, or aircraft piracy or the unlawful throwing, placing, or discharging of a destructive device or bomb.

(6) The capital felony was committed for pecuniary gain.

(7) The capital felony was committed to disrupt or hinder the lawful exercise of any governmental function or the enforcement of laws.

(8) The capital felony was committed against a law-enforcement officer, employee of the Department of Correction, jailer, fireman, judge or justice, former judge or justice, prosecutor or former prosecutor, juror or former juror, or witness or former witness against the defendant, while engaged in the performance of his official duties or because of the exercise of his official duty.

(9) The capital felony was especially heinous, atrocious, or cruel.

(10) The defendant knowingly created a great risk of death to more than one person by means of a weapon or device which would normally be hazardous to the lives of more than one person.

(11) The murder for which the defendant stands convicted was part of a course of conduct in which the defendant engaged and which included the commission by the defendant of other crimes of violence against another person or persons.

Mitigating circumstances are listed in NCGS §15A-2000(f). However, the statute does state that the jury is not limited to the mitigating circumstances listed in the statue, which include:

(1) The defendant has no significant history of prior criminal activity.

(2) The capital felony was committed while the defendant was under the influence of mental or emotional disturbance.

(3) The victim was a voluntary participant in the defendant's homicidal conduct or consented to the homicidal act.

(4) The defendant was an accomplice in or accessory to the capital felony committed by another person and his participation was relatively minor.

(5) The defendant acted under duress or under the domination of another person.

(6) The capacity of the defendant to appreciate the criminality of his conduct or to conform his conduct to the requirements of law was impaired.

(7) The age of the defendant at the time of the crime.

(8) The defendant aided in the apprehension of another capital felon or testified truthfully on behalf of the prosecution in another prosecution of a felony.

(9) Any other circumstance arising from the evidence which the jury deems to have mitigating value.

After the jury has heard all the evidence, arguments of counsel, and instructions by the court, and considered all aggravating and mitigating factors, they deliberate and render a recommendation to the court. The sentence recommendation must be unanimous and when the verdict is delivered to the court, each member of the jury is individually polled.[15] If the jury recommends the death penalty, the judge must impose a sentence of death. If the jury recommends a sentence of life imprisonment, the judge must impose a sentence of imprisonment for life without parole.[16] If the jury cannot come to unanimous agreement as to a sentencing recommendation, the judge may not impose the death penalty and must instead sentence the offender to life imprisonment.[17] In all cases in which an offender is sentenced to death, the judgment is automatically reviewed by the North Carolina Supreme Court.[18]

THE PROCEDURE FOR EXECUTIONS IN NORTH CAROLINA

All executions are held in a permanent death chamber located in the Central Prison, in Raleigh, North Carolina. The individuals who are allowed to be present at an execution are specified in NCGS §15-190. They include prison staff, official witnesses, members of the victim's family, and representatives of the offender being executed. Specifically, the statute states that the following individuals may be present at an execution

- the warden or deputy warden, or some other person designed by the warden to attend in the warden's place

- the surgeon or physician of the penitentiary

- four respectable citizens (who serve as official witnesses)

- two members of the victim's family

- the offender's legal counsel

- relatives of the offender

- a minister or member of the clergy or religious leader of the offender's choosing

No more than 16 individuals may witness the execution, due to space limitations in the witness viewing room.[19] In addition, five representatives from the media are selected to witness the execution and brief other members of the media on what they observed.[20]

As noted above, the only method of execution currently authorized in North Carolina is lethal injection, which is defined as "the administration of an ultrashort-acting barbiturate in combination with a chemical paralytic agent."[21] The process is described on the North Carolina Department of Correction website as follows:

> The inmate is secured with lined ankle and wrist restraints to a gurney in the preparation room outside the chamber. Cardiac monitor leads and a stethoscope are attached. Two saline intravenous lines are started, one in each arm, and the inmate is covered with a sheet.
>
> The inmate is given the opportunity to speak and pray with the chaplain. The warden then gives the condemned an opportunity to record a final statement that will be made public. After the witnesses are in place, the inmate's gurney is taken into the chamber by correctional officers who draw the curtain and exit. Appropriately trained personnel then enter behind the curtain and connect the cardiac monitor leads, the injection devices and the stethoscope to the appropriate leads. The warden informs the witnesses that the execution is about to begin. He returns to the chamber and gives the order to proceed.
>
> The saline intravenous lines are turned off and the thiopental sodium is injected which puts the inmate into a deep sleep. Potassium chloride is then injected, leading to cardiac arrest. An injection of pancuronium bromide follows. This agent is a total muscle relaxer. The inmate stops breathing and dies soon afterward.
>
> The warden pronounces the inmate dead and a physician certifies death has occurred. The witnesses are escorted to the elevators and the body is released to the medical examiner.[22]

The total cost of the supplies required for an execution by lethal injection is approximately $105.63 (depending on the supplier used, the current costs, and the amount of each drug that is actually used).[23]

NOTES

1.   North Carolina Department of Correction web site - The Death Penalty
      (http://www.doc.state.nc.us/DOP/deathpenalty/index.htm)
2.   *Furman v. Georgia*, 408 U.S. 238 (1972)
3.   *Woodson v. North Carolina*, 428 U.S. 280 (1976); see also the companion case of *Roberts v. Louisiana*, 428 U.S. 325 (1976)
4.   North Carolina Department of Correction web site, *op. cit.*
5.   *Ibid*
6.   Death Penalty Information Center home page (http://www.deathpenaltyinfo.org/index.php)
7.   North Carolina General Statutes, §14-17

8. North Carolina General Statutes, §15A-2005(b); see §15A-2005(a) for a definition of mental retardation in North Carolina
9. North Carolina Department of Correction web site, *op. cit.*
10. *Ibid*
11. *Ibid*
12. North Carolina General Statutes, §15A-2004(b)
13. North Carolina General Statutes, §15A-2004(c)
14. North Carolina General Statutes, §15A-2000(a)(4)
15. North Carolina General Statutes, §15A-2000(b)
16. North Carolina General Statutes, §15A-2002
17. North Carolina General Statutes, §15A-2000(b)
18. North Carolina General Statutes, §15A-2000(d)(1)
19. North Carolina Department of Correction web site, *op. cit.*
20. *Ibid*
21. North Carolina General Statutes, §15-187
22. North Carolina Department of Correction web site, *op. cit.*
23. *Ibid*

CHAPTER 8

CORRECTIONS IN NORTH CAROLINA

THE NORTH CAROLINA DEPARTMENT OF CORRECTION

The **North Carolina Department of Correction** (DOC) oversees the operation of all state correctional facilities in North Carolina. It was created in 1973 and given the duty to:

> provide the necessary custody, supervision, and treatment to control and rehabilitate criminal offenders and thereby to reduce the rate and cost of crime and delinquency.[1]

The DOC was originally created as the **Department of Social Rehabilitation and Control** and included not only prisons but also all probation, parole, and juvenile facilities. The department was renamed the DOC in 1974 and, in 1975, responsibility for juveniles was transferred to the Department of Human Resources.

The DOC is composed of five main divisions. The **Administration Division** is responsible for the daily organization, and essentially runs the DOC. It includes purchasing, research and planning, information systems management, and staff training and development. The **Division of Prisons** is responsible for over 70 correctional facilities spread throughout North Carolina. It includes sections that provide support services to these facilities, such as classification, housing, security, health, food, education, and rehabilitation programs. The **Division of Community Corrections** provides supervised community-based alternatives for offenders. The **Division of Alcohol and Chemical Dependency Programs** was created by GS §143B-262(1) and GS §143B-264, both of which state that the DOC "shall establish a substance abuse program." The Division provides a variety of programs to assist offenders in alcohol and drug recovery. Finally, the **Correction Enterprises Division** creates opportunities for inmates in prison to gain valuable work experience while at the same time providing a variety of goods and services to the state.[2]

In addition to these five divisions, there are two independent bodies attached to the DOC. These are the **Inmate Grievance and Resolution Board** and the **North Carolina Post-Release Supervision and Parole Commission**. Members of these bodies are appointed by the governor.

The DOC employs over 18,000 individuals. The agency's authorized budget during the 2001-2002 fiscal year was $960,071,979.[3]

PRISONS IN NORTH CAROLINA

Prisons in North Carolina are run by the DOC. As of May 9, 2003, there were 33,817 inmates in the North Carolina prison system, not including offenders on probation or parole. Of these inmates, 93 percent were male and 7 percent were female.[4] There are 76 state prisons in North Carolina as well as one private non-profit contracted facility.[5]

Prison Security Levels

Each prison facility in the state is given an individual **security level** designation based on the prison's physical structure and design, the type of cells, the level of staffing, and the type and intensity of staff supervision. There are three main custody levels: close custody, medium custody, and minimum custody. The higher the level of security, the more restrictive the confinement and the more separated offenders are from the community outside the facility.

Close Custody is the most restrictive level. It is used for offenders who have been convicted of very serious offenses, who are considered to be at risk of escape, or whose past behavior in prison has shown them to be disruptive and unwilling to follow institution rules. Close custody facilities generally are divided into cellblocks with single cells. Cell doors are opened and closed by remote control, from a secure control area in the cellblock. Each cell will contain a sink and toilet. Inmates in close custody facilities are under constant supervision by armed custody staff and their movement is restricted, although they are allowed to leave their cells to participate in work or other programs within the prison facility. There are 13 close custody facilities in North Carolina. Within some close custody facilities, some cell areas may be designated as **maximum security units**. These units contain single cells with remote controlled doors and house the most dangerous offenders, those who are a threat to the public, to other inmates, and to the staff of the facility. These offenders are usually confined within their cells 23 hours each day, with a one-hour shower and exercise period. Whenever an offender in a maximum security unit leaves the cell, s/he is physically restrained and escorted by one or more correctional officers.

Medium Custody facilities are less restrictive than close custody prisons, although inmates are still supervised by armed correctional officers. Medium custody prisons frequently use dormitory-style housing rather than cellblocks with single cells. Each dormitory may house up to 50 inmates and usually contains group toilet, sink, and shower facilities. Inmates sleep in double-decker bunk beds and each inmate has a metal locker for storage of clothing and other personal belongings. The movement of inmates within the facility is less controlled and supervised than in a close custody facility. Each facility also contains one unit made up of single cells which is used to punish inmates who violate the rules of the facility. Some inmates in medium custody facilities are allowed to work on road squads outside the walls of the prison, when supervised by armed correctional officers. There are 24 medium custody facilities in North Carolina.

Minimum Custody is the least restrictive and secure level. All misdemeanor offenders are placed in minimum custody and felony offenders may be moved ("promoted") to this custody level if it is considered appropriate. Offenders in minimum custody facilities are those who are believed to pose little risk to the public safety. These facilities generally use dormitory-style housing. There are three levels of minimum custody in North Carolina. Inmates in **Minimum Custody Level I** are allowed to work on the prison grounds or even away from the prison facility as long as they are supervised by a correctional officers. Inmates in **Minimum Custody Level II** may work on the prison grounds or away from the facility while under supervision by a supervisor from another government agency. These inmates may also be given a short-term furlough, or community pass, if accompanied by a certified community volunteer. Finally, inmates in **Minimum Custody Level III** are given the most freedom; they may be eligible for programs outside the facility, such as work, release, school release, or home leaves. There are 39 minimum custody facilities in North Carolina.

During FY 2001-2002, 37 percent of DOC inmates were placed in minimum custody facilities, 46 percent in medium custody facilities, and 17 percent in close custody institutions.[6]

In addition to the three main custody levels, an inmate may be assigned to a **control status** or **segregation**. These inmates are separated from the regular prison population. There are six main segregation assignments. **Disciplinary segregation** is commonly known as "lock-up". Inmates assigned to this status have been found guilty of violating a prison rule and are being punished. Inmates assigned to **administrative segregation** have been removed from the regular population for a temporary period to protect staff and/or other inmates or to provide order and control within the facility. Similarly, an inmate may be placed on **protective control** if the inmate may be placed in danger if not removed from the regular prison population. **Intensive control** is for those inmates who regularly or continually engage in disruptive and undisciplined behavior and regularly disturb the routine operation of the prison facility. **Maximum control** is more restrictive than intensive control and is for inmates who pose a continuing threat to the safety of prison staff and/or other inmates and to prison security. Finally, **high security maximum control** is for those inmates who pose the most serious threat to the facility and to the safety of staff and inmates. This is the most restrictive location in the entire DOC. Inmates on protective, intensive, maximum, or high security maximum control must have their status reviewed every six months.[7]

Classification of Inmates to Custody Levels

When an inmate is transferred to the DOC to begin serving a sentence of incarceration, s/he is first sent to a **prison receiving center** (or **reception center**) for processing, evaluation, and classification. There are 11 reception centers in North Carolina, seven for adult males, two for females, and two for male youth. The evaluation process includes medical, dental, and psychological health screening, and the collection of a wide variety of information about the offender (family history, educational history, work history, criminal history, job skills, etc.) This information is used to assign the offender to the appropriate custody level and the appropriate prison facility, and to determine if the inmate requires any special services (e.g., medical or mental health treatment). During this period the inmate will also go through an individual or group orientation to the DOC, learning about DOC rules, procedures, penalties and discipline, and other important information.

The inmate is initially classified to one of the prison custody levels and assigned to a specific facility. However, correctional staff continue to monitor the inmate's behavior and do regular risk assessments. Inmates who obey prison rules, perform assigned work tasks, and participate in rehabilitative and treatment programs may be moved to lower custody facilities, while those who violate prison rules may be punished and re-classified to a more restrictive and secure custody facility. Promotion to a less restrictive custody level is a privilege that must be earned by the offender.[8]

The Cost of Incarceration in a State Prison

The cost of incarcerating an offender in a state facility depends on the custody level. During FY 2001-2002, the average daily cost of incarcerating one inmate was $62.43. Broken down by custody level, the average daily cost was:

- minimum custody - $50.04
- medium custody - $65.17
- close custody - $80.19

These costs include not only the cost of supervising and housing inmates and providing programs and services, but also the indirect administrative costs for the DOC support of prison facilities.[9]

Who is in Prison in North Carolina?

All felony and misdemeanor offenders who receive a custodial sentence of at least 90 days are under the jurisdiction of the DOC. During FY 2001-2002, a total of 23, 760 offenders were admitted to prisons in the state. This is the largest number of admissions since FY 1994-1995. There are four main categories of admissions to prison. **New admissions** are those offenders who received a sentence of incarceration and are transferred to the custody of the DOC. **Probation revocations** and **parole/post-release supervision revocations** involve offenders who are brought or returned to prison because they have violated the conditions of probation, parole, or post-release supervision. These violations may include the commission of new crimes. Finally, **safekeepers** are defendants who have not yet been sentenced by the court but who are being held in a prison facility because it is felt that detaining them in a local jail places them in danger from other jail inmates or places others in the jail in jeopardy, or because the defendant requires medical care. The category of safekeepers also includes not only unconvicted defendants but also **pre-sentence diagnostic admissions**, defendants who have been convicted but not yet sentenced, because the judge has requested a diagnostic assessment from DOC prior to holding a sentencing hearing. During FY 2001-2002, 43 percent of all admissions were new admissions while 49 percent were probation revocations.[10]

Of the 6,746 misdemeanor admissions to the DOC in FY 2001-2002, approximately 44 percent were convicted of Class 1 misdemeanor offenses, such as non-trafficking drug offenses and breaking and entering. Approximately 33 percent of these offenders were convicted of DWI offenses. Almost 20 percent were convicted of Class A1 misdemeanors, primarily assaults.[11]

A total of 15,687 felony offenders were admitted to prison during FY 2001-2002. The vast majority (almost 79 percent) were for Class F, G, H, and I offenses. Almost 39 percent of the admissions were Class H felonies, such as breaking and entering, larceny, and non-trafficking drug offenses. The remaining 21 percent of the admissions were offenders committing more serious offenses, such as sexual assaults (Class B1), second degree murder (Class B2), habitual felon (Class C), robbery (Class D) and other violent personal crimes (primarily Class E). Less than 1 percent of all felony admissions were for a Class A felony (first degree murder).[12]

On June 30, 2002, there were a total of 33,021 offenders in the North Carolina prison system. Approximately 5 percent of the prison population are misdemeanor offenders. The remaining 95 percent are felony offenders. Approximately 55 percent of the prison population have been convicted of serious felony crimes (Class A through E offenses). Although only 21 percent of felony admissions were for these crimes, their representation in the prison population is so high because they receive lengthy sentences and therefore remain in the population for a long period of time. Similarly, although there were only 104 Class A felons admitted to prison during FY 2001-2001, there were 1,193 such offenders in the prison population at the end of the fiscal year. These offenders are either sentenced to life in prison or death.[13]

Of the offenders in custody on June 30, 2002, almost 94 percent were male and 6 percent were female. Approximately 63 percent of male inmates were black, 32 percent white, and the remaining 5 percent of other races. Among female inmates, approximately 49 percent were black, 46 percent white, and 4 percent of other races.[14]

During FY 2001-2002 there were a total of 86 escapes from DOC custody. The majority of these were offenders placed in minimum custody facilities; many did not return to prison on time from a work release job. However, as of December 2002, only five of these inmates had not been captured and returned to custody. Approximately 84 percent of all escapees were captured within one week of their escape. This includes approximately 50 percent who were captured the same day they escaped and an additional 24 percent who were captured the next day.[15]

A Day in a Close Custody Facility

The DOC website provides an outline of how offenders incarcerated in prison facilities of various custody levels spend a typical day.[16] In Central Prison, a close custody facility in Raleigh housing male offenders, inmates are never allowed to leave the prison grounds and movement within the prison is restricted. Inmates working in the kitchen are awakened at 3:30am to prepare breakfast. These inmates are housed together, are moved to and from the kitchen area as a group, and are thoroughly searched before being allowed to enter the kitchen. They arrive at the kitchen at 4am to begin preparing meals. The remainder of the inmates are awakened at 6:00am for the first formal count of the day. Breakfast begins at 7:00am and inmates assigned to the first shift of work must report to their jobs at 7:30am. Jobs include working in the kitchen, laundry, or license tag facility, performing janitorial tasks, or performing prison maintenance. Inmates receive a 30-minute lunch break at noon before returning to work.

The work-day ends at 3:00pm, when the inmate will usually go into the recreation yard. At 4:00pm inmates return to their cells for another formal count. Following this count, dinner is served and then the inmate may spend time in the recreation yard, gym, or auditorium, or participate in organized recreational activities. Non-contact visitation occurs four days a week; visits may last from 60 to 90 minutes.

Between 6:30pm and 8:30pm, inmates are given the opportunity to attend educational classes or participate in treatment or counseling programs (e.g., Alcoholics Anonymous, Narcotics Anonymous, anger management classes). At 8:30pm all inmates return to their cells for another formal count. When the count is completed, at approximately 9:00pm, inmates may congregate in group areas within a housing unit and watch television, play games, write letters, and so on. Inmates are locked in their individual cells at 11:00pm and the lights are dimmed for the night.

PRISON LABOR IN NORTH CAROLINA

A History of Prison Labor in North Carolina

Beginning in approximately 1875, North Carolina correctional institutions leased inmates to private employers to work as laborers, commonly on railroads or in rock quarries. Under the **leasing system**, the employer was fully responsible for the custody of the inmate. In 1901, the system was changed to one of **contract labor**. Under this system, inmates still worked for private employers but custody of the inmates was the responsibility of the prison. That same year, the state's **Good Roads Policy** used inmate labor to build roads throughout North Carolina. The inmates were housed in **prison cages** that were drawn by horses or mules and transported the inmates between road construction sites. As many as a dozen inmates slept in each cage. Despite the inhumane conditions in which inmates were forced to live, prison cages remained in regular use until 1933, when the state began to use **road camps** instead. In 1910, the state began an **incentive wage system** for inmates. Inmates received up to 15 cents a day for their labor; the wages were paid upon the inmate's release from prison.

In 1933, the state took over a number of road camps that had been operated at the county level. The camps were renovated and several additional camps were constructed. The camps were used to house inmates working on the building or repairing of roads. Each camp housed 100 inmates.

In the early 1930s, the state began developing **prison industries**. This program evolved into the current Correction Enterprises program. The first prison industry involved inmates making concrete pipes for the North Carolina State Highway Commission. Other industries developed over the years, including farming and tailoring. The first work release program was begun in 1957, allowing inmates to work privately outside the prison and spend the night in the prison facility. This was the first work release program in the United States.[17]

Prison Labor in North Carolina Today

According to GS §148-6,

> The State Department of Correction ... shall have full power and authority to provide for employment of such convicts, either in the prison or on farms leased or owned by the State of North Carolina, or elsewhere, or otherwise; and may contract for the hire or employment of any able-bodied convicts upon such terms as may be just and fair, but such convicts so hired, or employed, shall remain under the actual management, control and care of the Department: Provided, however, that no female convict shall be worked on public roads or streets in any manner.

Most North Carolina prison inmates work at some job, although the majority work inside prison facilities. Inmates receive incentive wages, which range from 40 cents to $1.00 per day, depending on the specific work assignment. During FY 2001-2002, an average of 17,309 inmates were given work assignments. Approximately 69 percent of these inmates worked within prisons, many of them engaged in the daily tasks of helping to run the prison facility. The remainder were given work assignments outside the prison facility.[18]

Work Activities in Prison Facilities

Many of the work assignments within prison facilities involve daily operational activities. These assignments often provide inmates with valuable job skills and work experience, as well as helping to reduce prison operating costs.

Over 25 percent of inmates given a work assignment were assigned to **Unit Services**. These inmates perform a wide variety of janitorial and general maintenance duties in the facility, helping to keep the prison running. Approximately 17 percent of working inmates are assigned to **Food Service**. They work in prison kitchens, preparing and serving food and learning useful job skills. Inmates may also be assigned to **Prison Maintenance** (which is separate from Unit Services). These inmates are involved in tasks such as light construction, roofing, plumbing, wiring, and grounds-keeping. Inmates who have prior skills and experience in **Construction** may be assigned to participate in the construction of new prison facilities.[19]

Correction Enterprises

The **Correction Enterprises** division of the DOC administers prison industries within close and medium custody prison facilities. Inmates learn job skills that will help them obtain employment when released from prison. Correction Enterprise jobs provide incentive wages of up to $3 per day, depending on the skills needed to perform the job. Inmates also may receive earned time toward a reduction of their maximum sentence length. Over 2,000 inmates are employed in Correction Enterprises activities.

There are a wide variety of work opportunities. The North Carolina Correctional Center for Women houses a license plate plant, making not only all state standard and specialty license plates but also a wide variety of local tags and other speciality items Inmates at Nash Correctional Institution and Franklin Correctional Center make street and highway signs. Correction Enterprises operates a print shop at Nash Correctional Institution that employs approximately 100 inmates. Other programs include a duplicating plant, a paint plant, several metal products plants, several sewing plants, an upholstery and woodworking plant, a meat processing plant, a janitorial products plant, and a cannery. Several work farms are also run by Correction Enterprises. Other services include laundries, warehouses, manpower services, and forestry operations. Recently, Correction Enterprises opened a new optical plant.

Products and services provided by Correction Enterprises inmates include:

- stainless steel kitchen equipment
- lockers and bunks

- office furniture
- mattresses for prison use
- uniforms for inmates and officers
- bed and bath linens
- janitorial products
- traffic and architectural paint
- vegetable canning and meat repackaging for use in prison kitchens
- farming operations
- laundry services for state prisons, hospitals, and some state agencies
- printing and duplicating services for local and state governments[20]

Work Activities Outside Prison Facilities

Inmates in minimum and medium custody facility may be allowed to participate in work activities outside the prison facility. Over 2,000 inmates work on **road squads**. They pick up litter, patch potholes, and clear right-of-ways. Minimum custody inmates are under the direction of employees from the Department of Transportation while medium custody inmates are supervised by armed correctional officers.[21]

The **Governor's Community Work Program** began in 1994. It uses minimum custody offenders for short-term manual labor projects for local communities and state agencies. Local communities have labor contracts with the DOC and provide all necessary materials but are not charged for the inmate labor. Activities include picking up litter, cleaning and painting buildings, cleaning school busses, cleaning up after a hurricane, and so on. Inmates work in squads of up to 10 and are supervised by a correctional officer. Local governments may also contract with the DOC to have inmates work on longer-term projects, such as recycling projects or clerical activities. In 2001, inmates on community work crews totaled almost 2.3 million hours of work. Based on a minimum hourly wage of $5.15, the estimated value of the inmate labor is over $12 million.[22]

A small percentage of minimum custody inmates are allowed to participate in **work release**. They are generally nearing their release date and are allowed to leave the prison facility and work for a business in the community. Inmates who are on work release receive wages from their employers at the prevailing rate but are required to pay room and board to the prison. Wages are also used towards payment of fines and victim restitution and to support the inmate's family.[23]

JAILS IN NORTH CAROLINA

In North Carolina, the primary difference between a **jail** and a **prison** is that prisons are usually run by the state whereas jails, or **local confinement facilities**, are managed by the county or local municipality. GS §153A-218 gives any county in North Carolina the authority to "establish, acquire, erect, repair, maintain, and operate local confinement facilities and may for these purposes appropriate funds not otherwise limited as to use by law." The statute does not mandate a jail but it is clear from this and other statutes that counties are responsible for providing a local confinement facility. In some cases, two or more counties have agreed to share a single district or regional jail, as authorized by GS §153A-219. For example, Martin County and Bertie County have a joint venture for a regional jail operated by the Bertie-Martin Regional Jail Commission.

According to the General Assembly, local confinement facilities in North Carolina should

> provide secure custody of persons confined therein in order to protect the community and should be operated so as to protect the health and welfare of prisoners and provide for their humane treatment.[24]

County jails are operated by the Board of County Commissioners and by the county sheriff. The Board's main responsibility is to pay for the construction and operation of the jail while the sheriff is responsible for the day-to-day management of the jail. GS §162-22 states that "The sheriff shall have the care and custody of the jail in his county; and shall be, or appoint, the keeper thereof." Because this statute specifically gives the care and custody of the jail over to the sheriff, counties in North Carolina are not allowed to privatize jails without specific authorization from the General Assembly.

The majority of inmates in county jails are pretrial detainees and convicted offenders serving short terms of incarceration, usually for misdemeanors. **Pretrial detainees** are defendants who are held in confinement while awaiting trial, generally because they do not satisfy the conditions of pretrial release that were set by the magistrate or judge. For example, a defendant's release order may require pretrial release upon payment of a specified amount of money (a bond). However, until the defendant is able to obtain the required amount of money, or arrange for a bail bondsman to secure the bond, s/he will be detained in the county jail.

The majority of **convicted offenders** in county jails were specifically ordered by the court to serve their terms in such a facility. However, a small number of offenders who have been sentenced to a term of incarceration to be served in a state prison may be held temporarily in a county jail until a space in a state prison becomes available. Most offenders sentenced to terms of incarceration in county jails were convicted of misdemeanor offenses, generally with a sentence length of 90 days or less. Misdemeanor offenders given sentences of more than 90 days may be sent either to a jail or to DOC. All felony offenders must be committed to the custody of the DOC.

In addition, some inmates may be confined in a county jail because of **contempt of court**. **Civil contempt** involves an individual failing to comply with a court order when s/he is capable of doing so. A person found in civil contempt by the court may be placed in a county jail until s/he is willing to comply with the court order. **Criminal contempt** involves deliberate disobedience of a court order or showing disrespect to the court during proceedings. Criminal contempt is punishable by imprisonment in a county jail for up to 30 days.

In North Carolina, jails are on occasion also used to care for **intoxicated individuals**. For example, according to GS §122C-303,

> An officer may assist an individual found intoxicated in a public place by directing or transporting that individual to a city or county jail. That action may be taken only if the intoxicated individual is apparently in need of and apparently unable to

provide for himself food, clothing, or shelter but is not apparently in need of immediate medical care and if no other facility is readily available to receive him ... The intoxicated individual may be detained at the jail only until he becomes sober or a maximum of 24 hours and may be released at any time to a relative or other individual willing to be responsible for his care.

Finally, some **federal inmates** may be confined in a county jail if space permits. These individuals are usually awaiting processing for federal criminal charges. The federal government is required to reimburse the county for expenses related to the confinement of the offender.[25]

COMMUNITY SUPERVISION IN NORTH CAROLINA

Offenders placed on any form of community supervision are the responsibility of the DOC's **Division of Community Corrections** (DCC). The DCC is divided into four judicial divisions. There are 273 field offices throughout the state, with 2,137 certified officers who monitor the behavior of offenders who are on probation, parole, or post-release supervision and provide referrals to various services and programs.[26]

The cost of supervising offenders in the community is significantly lower than the cost of prison incarceration. The actual costs, including both direct supervision costs and indirect costs relating to administration of the DCC, vary depending on the type of supervision being provided. For example, during FY 2001-2002, the average daily cost of supervising an offender placed on regular community supervision (probation or parole) was $1.83, the cost of supervising an offender on electronic house arrest averaged $7.92 per day, and an offender on intensive supervision cost an average of $11.47 per day. As noted above, the average daily cost of incarcerating an offender in a minimum custody DOC facility was $50.04.[27] As of June 30, 2002, the DCC was supervising a total of 117,374 offenders. Approximately 97 percent of these offenders were on probation, two percent were on parole, and slightly less than 1 percent were on post-release supervision.[28]

Parole

Parole is not in itself a sentence. It is a form of early supervised release from a sentence of incarceration. Parole was essentially eliminated in North Carolina when the General Assembly adopted the Structured Sentencing Law in 1993. However, some offenders are still eligible for parole, including those who were sentenced prior to the adoption of structured sentencing. In addition, parole is still used for offenders who were convicted of impaired driving (DWI).[29] As a result, the population of offenders on parole has declined significantly; between 1997 and 2002, the number of offenders on parole decreased by approximately two-thirds.[30] On June 30, 2002, approximately 24 percent of offenders in prison were not sentenced under structured sentencing laws. Therefore, parole will continue to be used in North Carolina for some time. However, the decrease in the parole population is expected to continue.[31]

On June 30, 2002 there were 2,276 offenders being supervised on parole. Of these, 38 percent had been convicted of public order crimes (primarily drug offenses and driving while impaired). Approximately 33 percent of paroled offenders had been convicted of crimes against persons, including robbery, assault, and second degree murder. Approximately 26 percent had been convicted of property crimes, particularly larceny, burglary, breaking and entering, and fraud. Information on the underlying crime was missing for 3 percent of the parole population.[32]

The **North Carolina Post-Release Supervision and Parole Commission** is responsible for determining who is released on parole, based on statutory eligibility requirements. It is composed of three members, who are appointed by the Governor. A majority vote of the Commission is required for all parole decisions. Factors considered by the Commission when determining whether an offender should be granted or denied parole include the crime committed, prior criminal history, conduct while in prison, participation in prison programs, and information from victims, court officials, and others.[33]

If parole is granted, the Commission sets the length of a parole term and imposes conditions of parole. Offenders may not serve a term of parole longer than one year.[34] While on parole, the offender may be required to comply with a variety of conditions. One condition that must be imposed upon all parolees is that the parolee may not commit another crime during the parole period.[35] Other conditions may be imposed at the discretion of the Commission. GS §1374(b) lists appropriate conditions that may be imposed upon a parolee. These include:

- the offender must work or attend school/vocational training
- the offender must undergo available medical/psychiatric treatment
- the offender must attend or live in a facility for parolees that provides rehabilitation, instruction, recreation, etc.
- the offender must support dependents and meet family responsibilities
- the offender may not own a firearm or other dangerous weapon without permission
- the offender must report to a parole officer regularly
- the offender must permit a parole officer to visit him or her at home or at other locations
- the offender must stay within a specified geographic region unless given permission to leave
- the offender may not move or change jobs without prior approval from a parole officer
- the offender must allow himself or herself to be searched by a parole officer at reasonable times
- the offender must make restitution or reparation
- the offender must continue attending a GED program
- the offender must satisfy any other conditions imposed by the Commission that are reasonably related to his or her rehabilitation

Post-Release Supervision

The passage of the Structured Sentencing Law created a new type of community supervision known as **post-release supervision**. Post-release supervision is defined as:

> The time for which a sentenced prisoner is released from prison before the termination of his maximum prison term, controlled by the rules and conditions of this Article. Purposes of post-release supervision include all or any of the following:

to monitor and control the prisoner in the community, to assist the prisoner in reintegrating into society, to collect restitution and other court indebtedness from the prisoner, and to continue the prisoner's treatment or education.[36]

An offender must serve the minimum term of imprisonment imposed by the court before release from prison. According to GS §15A-1368.2(a),

> A prisoner to whom this Article applies shall be released from prison for post-release supervision on the date equivalent to his maximum imposed prison term less nine months, less any earned time awarded by the Department of Correction or the custodian of a local confinement facility ... If a prisoner has not been awarded any earned time, the prisoner shall be released for post-release supervision on the date equivalent to his maximum prison term less nine months.

The statute also states that a prisoner may not refuse post-release supervision.[37] For most offenders, the period of post-release supervision is nine months, although in some cases the term of supervision may be for up to five years.[38] The **North Carolina Post-Release Supervision and Parole Commission** is responsible for determining post-release supervision conditions. Approved post-release supervision conditions are similar to those imposed upon parolees and are discussed in GS §15A-1368.4.

The number of offenders entering post-release supervision has increased steadily and significantly since 1996, due to the use of structured sentencing. In FY 1996-1997, 83 offenders entered post-release supervision; during FY 2001-2002, this number increased to 1,151. This number is expected to continue to increase as more offenders sentenced under structured sentencing become eligible for post-release supervision. FY 2001-2002 was the first year that offenders convicted of Class B2 crimes entered post-release, while no Class B1 offenders have yet been released because of their long sentences. Of those offenders on post-release supervision on June 30, 2002, the majority (approximately 57 percent) had been convicted of Class E offenses, especially assaults, kidnapping, robbery, sexual assault, and manslaughter.[39]

Probation

Unlike parole or post-release supervision, **probation** is a sentence imposed by the court. The sentence is served in the community, rather than in a prison or jail, and the offender is supervised and required to abide by various conditions. Under the Structured Sentencing Law, the length of a period of probation is set by statute. For example, a term of probation for misdemeanor offenders receiving a sentence of community punishment must be between six and 18 months. For misdemeanor offenders receiving a sentence of intermediate punishment, a term of probation must be between 12 and 24 months. Felony offenders sentenced to community punishment may receive a term of probation between 12 and 30 months while those felony offenders receiving a sentence of intermediate punishment may receive a term of probation between 18 and 36 months. The court is allowed to exceed the maximum periods specified but may not sentence any offender to probation for longer than five years.[40]

Offenders placed on probation may be required to comply with a variety of conditions imposed by the court. These include both regular and special conditions. Regular conditions are imposed upon all probationers and include the following:

- the offender must not commit any new crimes
- the offender must remain within a specified jurisdiction unless given permission to leave
- the offender must report to a probation officer as directed by the court and must allow the probation officer to visit him or her at home or at other locations
- the offender must pay child support and satisfy other family obligations
- the offender may not possess a firearm or other deadly weapon without permission from the court
- the offender must pay a supervision fee
- the offender must remain employed or in school
- the offender must tell the probation officer if s/he fails to obtain or keep satisfactory employment
- the offender must pay any court costs and fines, and make restitution or reparation
- pay the state for the costs of appointed counsel, public defender or appellate defender.[41]

In addition, the court may choose to impose one or more special conditions on the probationer. Examples of special conditions of probation include, but are not limited to,

- requiring the offender to undergo medical and/or psychiatric treatment
- requiring the offender to attend or live in a facility that provides rehabilitation, counseling, treatment, social skills, or employment training
- requiring the offender to successfully complete a drug treatment court program
- requiring the offender to remain at home wearing an electronic monitoring device unless authorized to leave for the purpose of work, school, training, or counseling
- requiring the offender to turn in his or her driver's license and not operate a motor vehicle for a specified period of time
- perform community service.[42]

There are also a number of special rules and conditions that apply specifically to offenders sentenced under the Structured Sentencing Act.[43]

The number of offenders entering probation has increased steadily since the Structured Sentencing Act was adopted. During FY 2001-2001, there were a total of 62,746 new offender entries. Approximately 73 percent of these entries were for misdemeanor offenders; the remaining 27 percent were felons. The majority of offenders entering probation (53 percent) were convicted of public order crimes, especially drug offenses and traffic violations. Approximately 30 percent of probationers were convicted of property crimes, particularly larceny, breaking and entering, fraud, and forgery. Only 16 percent of all new probation entries were convicted of crimes against persons. The most common offenses were assaults, sexual offenses, and robbery.[44]

One special condition of probation that may be imposed is that of **electronic house arrest**. Offenders on electronic house arrest are confined to their place of residence and required to wear a special electronic monitoring device that allows the probation officer to monitor the offender's whereabouts. In general, electronic house arrest will be imposed for a period of one to three months. Offenders on house arrest may only leave their homes to go to work or school, to participate in court-mandated community service activities, or under other specific conditions which are approved by the probation officer.[45]

NOTES

1.   North Carolina General Statutes, §143B-261

2.   North Carolina Department of Correction home page (http://www.doc.state.nc.us/)

3.   North Carolina Department of Correction (2003, March). *Annual Statistical Report: Fiscal Year 2001-2002.* (http://crrp41.doc.state.nc.us/docs/pubdocs/0005567.PDF)

4.   North Carolina Department of Correction home page, *op. cit.*

5.   North Carolina Department of Correction (2003, March). *Annual Statistical Report: Fiscal Year 2001-2002.*

6.   *Ibid*

7.   North Carolina Department of Correction, Division of Prisons. *Handbook for Family and Friends of Inmates.* (http://www.doc.state.nc.us/Publications/fam_handbook.pdf)

8.   North Carolina Department of Correction (2003, March). *Annual Statistical Report: Fiscal Year 2001-2002.*

9.   *Ibid*

10.   *Ibid*

11.   *Ibid*

12.   *Ibid*

13.   *Ibid*

14.   *Ibid*

15.   *Ibid*

16.   North Carolina Department of Correction home page, *op. cit.*

17.   *Ibid*

18.   North Carolina Department of Correction (2003, March), *op. cit.*

19.   *Ibid*

20.   North Carolina Department of Correction home page, *op. cit.*

21.   North Carolina Department of Correction (2003, March), *op. cit.*

22.   North Carolina Department of Correction home page, *op. cit.*

23.   North Carolina Department of Correction (2003, March), *op. cit.*

24.   North Carolina General Statutes, §153A-216(1)

25.   North Carolina General Statutes, §162-34

26.   North Carolina Department of Correction home page, *op. cit.*

27.   North Carolina Department of Correction (2003, March), *op. cit.*

28.   North Carolina Division of Community Corrections (2003). *Annual Report: 2001-2002.* (http://www.doc.state.nc.us/dcc/annualreport/01-02annual_report.pdf)

29.   North Carolina General Statutes, §15A-1370.1

30.   North Carolina Division of Community Corrections (2003), *op. cit.*

31. North Carolina Department of Correction (2003, March), *op. cit.*
32. *Ibid*
33. North Carolina Department of Correction home page, *op. cit.*
34. North Carolina General Statutes, §15A-1372
35. North Carolina General Statutes, §15A-1374(a)
36. North Carolina General Statutes, §15A-1368(a)(1)
37. North Carolina General Statutes, §15A-1368.2(b)
38. North Carolina General Statutes, §15A-1368.2(c)
39. North Carolina Department of Correction (2003, March), *op. cit.*
40. North Carolina General Statutes, §15A-1343.2(d)
41. North Carolina General Statutes, §15A-1343(b)
42. North Carolina General Statutes, §15A-1343(b1)
43. North Carolina General Statutes, §15A-1343.2
44. North Carolina Department of Correction (2003, March), *op. cit.*
45. North Carolina Department of Correction home page, *op. cit.*

CHAPTER 9

THE JUVENILE JUSTICE SYSTEM
IN NORTH CAROLINA

INTRODUCTION

The definition of **juvenile** in North Carolina is found in the **Juvenile Code**, Chapter 7B of the North Carolina General Statutes. Subchapter II of the Juvenile Code deals specifically with undisciplined and delinquent juveniles. NCGS §1501(17) states that:

> Juvenile — Except as provided in subdivisions (7) and (27) of this section, any person who has not reached the person's eighteenth birthday and is not married, emancipated, or a member of the armed forces of the United States.

Subdivision 7 defines a **delinquent juvenile** as:

> Any juvenile who, while less than 16 years of age but at least 6 years of age, commits a crime or infraction under State law or under an ordinance of local government, including violation of the motor vehicle laws.

Subdivision 27 defines an **undisciplined juvenile** as:

> a. A juvenile who, while less than 16 years of age but at least 6 years of age, is unlawfully absent from school; or is regularly disobedient to and beyond the disciplinary control of the juvenile's parent, guardian, or custodian; or is regularly found in places where it is unlawful for a juvenile to be; or has run away from home for a period of more than 24 hours; or
> b. A juvenile who is 16 or 17 years of age and who is regularly disobedient to and beyond the disciplinary control of the juvenile's parent, guardian, or custodian; or is regularly found in places where it is unlawful for a juvenile to be; or has run away from home for a period of more than 24 hours.

Essentially, a delinquent juvenile is someone between the ages of 6 and 16 who has committed an act that would be a violation of the law it committed by an adult. An undisciplined juvenile, on the other hand, is a juvenile who has committed a **status offense**, or an act that is only an offense when it is committed by a juvenile.

THE NORTH CAROLINA DEPARTMENT OF JUVENILE JUSTICE AND DELINQUENCY PREVENTION

In 1998, the General Assembly enacted the **Juvenile Justice Reform Act**, a complete revision and restructuring of North Carolina laws relating to juveniles. The new Juvenile Code, Chapter 7B of the North Carolina General Statutes, became effective on July 1, 1999. It applies only to acts that were committed on or after that date. Thus, for example, a juvenile who committed a delinquent act on June 30, 1999 would fall under the old juvenile code[1]; if a juvenile committed a delinquent act on July 1, 1999, s/he would be dealt with under the new code.

Prior to the passage of the Act, two separate agencies shared responsibilities for juvenile justice functions. The Department of Health and Human Services Division of Youth Services was responsible for juvenile detention facilities and community based treatment while the Administrative Office of the Courts Juvenile Services Division was responsible for services such as screening, intake, probation, and post-release aftercare. However, the Act created a new agency, the **North Carolina Department of Juvenile Justice and Delinquency Prevention** (DJJDP), effective January 1, 1999. All responsibilities for juvenile justice functions were transferred to the DJJDP.[2] The DJJDP is headed by a Secretary who is appointed by the governor and who is responsible for the planning and management of all services and programs within the state's juvenile justice system.[3]

The DJJDP is organized around six main divisions. The **Administration Division** is responsible for the organization and management of the DJJDP, including policy development, employee training, public relations, and legislative reports. The **Deputy Secretary's Office** is the support center for the DJJDP, including managing the Department's budget, payroll, accounting, and other fiscal matters. This office is also responsible for maintenance and upkeep of existing facilities and for new construction. The **Intervention and Prevention Division** is responsible for providing intake, probation, and post-release services for delinquent and undisciplined juveniles. The **Youth Development Division** operates five youth development centers located around the state. These serve juveniles between the ages of 10 and 18 who have been adjudicated delinquent by the juvenile court system and committed to a youth development center for a term of at least six months. While in the center, juveniles participate in treatment, rehabilitation, education, and vocational programs. Violent juvenile offenders may remain in a youth development until age 19 or 20, depending on the offense. The **Human Resources Division** provides a variety of personnel services, including recruitment, salary and benefits administration, performance evaluations, and employee relations. Finally, the **Center for the Prevention of School Violence** serves as a resource center for efforts focused on improving school safety in the state, reducing fear, and encouraging positive youth development.[4]

WHAT HAPPENS TO A JUVENILE WHO IS ARRESTED IN NORTH CAROLINA

The juvenile justice system differs in several key ways from the adult criminal justice system.[5] After a juvenile is taken into custody by the police, s/he is referred to the DJJDP and goes through an **intake process**. The purpose of this process is:

to determine from available evidence whether there are reasonable grounds to believe the facts alleged are true, to determine whether the facts alleged constitute a delinquent or undisciplined offense within the jurisdiction of the court, to determine whether the facts alleged are sufficiently serious to warrant court action, and to obtain assistance from community resources when court referral is not necessary...[6]

Based on the offense of which the juvenile is accused, the intake counselor will classify the juvenile as either **divertible or non-divertible**. Divertible offenses include all undisciplined acts, all misdemeanors, and some felonies. In these cases, the counselor has the option of diverting the juvenile out of the juvenile court system. The counselor will develop a diversion plan, which may include any or all of the following:

- requiring the juvenile to make restitution
- requiring the juvenile to perform community service
- requiring the juvenile to go through victim-offender mediation
- requiring the juvenile to go through a physical training program
- requiring the juvenile to participate in a counseling program
- requiring the juvenile to participate in a teen court program

The diversion plan may include a diversion contract between the counselor, the juvenile, and the parent or guardian. The diversion contract includes:

- the conditions the juvenile agrees to abide by
- any actions the juvenile agrees to take
- any conditions the parent or guardian agrees to abide by
- any actions the parent or guardian agrees to take
- the role of the court counselor
- the length of the contract (no more than six months)
- an understanding that a violation of the contract by the juvenile may result in a petition being filed by the court
- an understanding that successful completion of the contract will prevent a petition being filed with the court.

If the juvenile fails to comply with the diversion plan developed by the counselor, a petition will be filed and the juvenile will be processed through the juvenile justice system.[7]

Non-divertible offenses include the following crimes:

- murder
- first or second degree rape
- first or second degree sexual offense
- arson
- felony drug offenses
- first degree burglary
- crimes against nature

- any felony involving the willful infliction of serious bodily injury or which involved the use of a deadly weapon[8]

If the intake counselor finds that there are reasonable grounds to believe that the juvenile has committed a non-divertible offense, s/he may not divert the juvenile from court. The counselor is required to authorize a **petition** to be filed with the juvenile court. A petition may also be filed on a divertible offense if the intake counselor chooses, or if a juvenile was diverted but failed to follow through with the diversion plan.

If a juvenile is alleged to be delinquent or undisciplined, s/he may be either detained by the DJJDP or released to the custody of a parent or guardian. Juveniles may be held in either secure or non-secure custody. **Non-secure custody** generally refers to some type of foster home placement and is used for some undisciplined and delinquent juveniles. **Secure custody** refers to a DJJDP detention facility and is used primarily for delinquent juveniles, as well as some undisciplined juveniles who meet certain criteria, as outlined in NCGS §7B-1903. No juvenile who has been alleged delinquent may be held in secure custody for more than five days or non-secure custody for more than seven days without a court hearing before a judge.[9]

If the delinquency petition alleges that the juvenile committed an offense that, if committed by an adult, would be a felony, the juvenile will proceed to a **first appearance hearing**. This must occur within ten days after the petition is filed with the court. NCGS §7B-1808 discusses the duties of the court during the first appearance. These include:

- informing the juvenile of the allegations outlined in the petition filed with the court

- determining whether the juvenile has retained or been assigned counsel

- informing the juvenile of the date of the probable cause hearing (within 15 days of the first appearance), if one is scheduled

- inform the juvenile's parent, guardian, or custodian of his/her responsibility to attend all scheduled hearings and explain that s/he may be held in contempt of court for failing to attend any hearing

If the juvenile is in either secure or non-secure custody, the first appearance generally will take place at the same time as the first custody hearing, which is held to determine the need for continued custody.

In any felony case involving a juvenile who was at least 13 years of age at the time of the commission of the offense, the court is required to conduct a **probable cause hearing** no more than 15 days after the first appearance. The juvenile is represented by counsel at this hearing. The purpose of the probable cause hearing is to determine whether there is probable cause to believe that the offense was actually committed and that the juvenile committed the offense.[10]

If the court finds that there is probable cause to believe the juvenile committed the alleged offense, the court will hold a **transfer hearing** to consider whether or not to transfer the juvenile to superior court for trial as an adult. Factors that are considered in the decision include:

- the age and maturity of the juvenile
- the juvenile's intellectual functioning
- the juvenile's prior record
- any prior attempts at rehabilitation
- any programs or facilities available to the court and the probability that the juvenile would benefit from participation in these programs
- the seriousness of the offense
- whether the protection of society requires that the juvenile be tried as an adult[11]

If the crime of which the juvenile is accused is a Class A felony, and probable cause is found, the court is required to **transfer** the case to the superior court if the juvenile is at least 13 years of age.[12] Juveniles transferred to adult court are given all the constitutional rights of any adult and may be sent to prison if convicted.

If the juvenile is not transferred to adult court, s/he will proceed to an **adjudication hearing**. The purpose of this hearing is to determine whether the allegations made against the juvenile are true. According to NCGS §7B-2403, "The adjudicatory hearing shall be held within a reasonable time in the district at the time and place the chief district court judge designates." Juveniles at an adjudication hearing have the following rights:

(1) The right to written notice of the facts alleged in the petition;
(2) The right to counsel;
(3) The right to confront and cross-examine witnesses;
(4) The privilege against self-incrimination;
(5) The right of discovery; and
(6) All rights afforded adult offenders except the right to bail, the right of self-representation, and the right of trial by jury.[13]

The level of proof required in an adjudication hearing is the same as that required in an adult trial: proof beyond a reasonable doubt.[14] If the court finds that the allegations set forth in the petition were not proved beyond a reasonable doubt, the juvenile is immediately released from custody (if s/he was being held in secure or non-secure custody) and is no longer under the jurisdiction of the juvenile justice system.[15] However, if the court finds that the allegations have been proved, the juvenile is adjudicated delinquent and may be held in custody while awaiting **disposition** of the case.

If a juvenile is adjudicated delinquent, the court may order a **predisposition investigation** to be conducted and a **predisposition report** prepared. This report, which may not be considered by the court until after adjudication, includes a risk and needs assessment that contains information on "the juvenile's social, medical, psychiatric, psychological, and educational history, as well as any factors indicating the probability of the juvenile committing further delinquent acts..."[16]

117

The next step for the juvenile adjudicated delinquent is a **dispositional hearing**. According to NCGS §7B-2500,

> The purpose of dispositions in juvenile actions is to design an appropriate plan to meet the needs of the juvenile and to achieve the objectives of the State in exercising jurisdiction, including the protection of the public. The court should develop a disposition in each case that:
> (1) Promotes public safety;
> (2) Emphasizes accountability and responsibility of both the parent, guardian, or custodian and the juvenile for the juvenile's conduct; and
> (3) Provides the appropriate consequences, treatment, training, and rehabilitation to assist the juvenile toward becoming a nonoffending, responsible, and productive member of the community.

There are a number of possible dispositional options or alternatives available to the court when dealing with a delinquent juvenile. The court selects the option that is most likely to protect the public, to meet the needs of the juvenile, and to be in the juvenile's best interests. Factors that the court considers include:

(1) The seriousness of the offense;
(2) The need to hold the juvenile accountable;
(3) The importance of protecting the public safety;
(4) The degree of culpability indicated by the circumstances of the particular case; and
(5) The rehabilitative and treatment needs of the juvenile indicated by a risk and needs assessment.[17]

NCGS §7B02506 lists a total of 24 possible dispositional alternatives. Examples include various types of custodial and non-custodial supervision, requiring the juvenile to pay a fine, make restitution, or perform community service, and the imposition of a curfew on the juvenile.

CUSTODIAL FACILITIES OPERATED BY DJJDP

DJJDP operates several types of custodial facilities for juveniles in North Carolina. These include detention centers, youth development centers, and wilderness camps.

A **detention center** is "a secure temporary facility where a juvenile will stay while waiting to go to court or until a placement can be arranged."[18] In 2001, a total of 6,778 juveniles between the ages of 7 and 18 were admitted to detention centers. Approximately 72 percent were male and 28 percent female. By race, approximately 54 percent were black and 40 percent white. The average length of stay was 10 days.[19]

A **youth development center** (YDC) serve juveniles who have been adjudicated delinquent and ordered by the court to such a center. To be placed in a YDC, a juvenile must be at least ten years of age. Terms of commitment are for a minimum of six months.[20] Services provided by YDCs include educational, vocational, recreational, and medical programs of various types. There are five

YDCs in North Carolina. During 2001, a total of 661 juveniles between the ages of 10 and 17 were admitted to YDCs. Approximately 87 percent were male and 13 percent female. Approximately 66 percent were black. and 28 percent were white.[21]

DJJDP also operates a **wilderness camp** known as Camp Woodson. Juveniles placed in YDCs may be eligible for participation in Camp Woodson. The program has two main purposes. First, it serves as a "short term, voluntary, pre-release program for juveniles returning to their home community on Conditional Release."[22] Second, the courts may require a juvenile to attend Camp Woodson as a condition of probation. The program is a true "camp" setting, so the juveniles live outdoors regardless of the weather. They participate in a variety of outdoor activities such as whitewater canoeing, rock climbing, horseback riding, backpacking, and community service. The camp runs eight sessions each year, each lasting 32 days, with a maximum of 15 juveniles per session.[23]

NOTES

1. The former juvenile code, now repealed, was Subchapter XI of North Carolina General Statutes Chapter 7A
2. North Carolina Department of Juvenile Justice and Delinquency Prevention home page (http://www.juvjus.state.nc.us/home/index.htm)
3. North Carolina General Statutes, §143B-516(a)
4. DJJDP home page, *op. cit.*
5. For a flowchart showing the juvenile justice process in North Carolina, see http://www.ncdjjdp.org/interprev_services/pdf/flowchart.pdf
6. North Carolina General Statutes, §7B-1700
7. North Carolina General Statutes, §7B-1706
8. North Carolina General Statutes, §7B-1701
9. North Carolina General Statutes, §7B-1906
10. North Carolina General Statutes, §7B-2202
11. North Carolina General Statutes, §7B-2203(b)
12. North Carolina General Statutes, §7B-2200
13. North Carolina General Statutes, §7B-2405
14. North Carolina General Statutes, §7B-2409
15. North Carolina General Statutes, §7B-2411
16. North Carolina General Statutes, §7B-2413
17. North Carolina General Statutes, §7B-2501
18. DJJDP home page, *op. cit.*
19. *Ibid*
20. North Carolina General Statutes, §7B-2513
21. DJJDP home page, *op. cit.*
22. *Ibid*
23. *Ibid*

CHAPTER 10

DRUGS AND CRIME IN NORTH CAROLINA

INTRODUCTION

Drug abuse is a serious problem in North Carolina. During 2001, there were 41,063 drug arrests in the state. Of these, almost 84 percent were for possession of illegal drugs, especially possession of marijuana, and the rest were for the sale and/or manufacture of illegal drugs.[1] Approximately 90 percent of these arrested were adults aged 18 or older. Juveniles were most commonly arrested for possession of marijuana.[2]

Drug and alcohol use is a serious issue among juveniles in North Carolina. In a 2001 survey conducted by the Centers for Disease Control and Prevention, approximately 38 percent of high school students surveyed admitted to drinking alcohol within the past month. 40 percent of those surveyed reported that they had used marijuana at least once during their lifetimes and 21 percent admitted to using marijuana within the past month. Almost 7 percent had used cocaine at least once. Approximately 33 percent of all juveniles surveyed reported that they were offered, sold, or given an illegal drug during the past 12 months by someone on school property.[3]

THE AVAILABILITY OF DRUGS IN NORTH CAROLINA

Marijuana

According to the U.S. Drug Enforcement Administration (DEA), **marijuana** is readily available in North Carolina. The majority is transported into the state after being smuggled across the U.S./Mexican border, but marijuana is also grown in the state.[4] During 2001, the North Carolina State Highway Patrol seized over 1,400 kilograms of marijuana.[5]

Cocaine

Cocaine, which is grown in Bolivia, Colombia, and Peru, is available in North Carolina. It is frequently smuggled into the United States from Mexico and transported to North Carolina by couriers. The DEA considers crack cocaine to be North Carolina's most serious drug-related problem.[6] During 2001, the North Carolina State Highway Patrol seized over 3,300 grams of cocaine.[7]

Heroin

Heroin is not a major problem in North Carolina, except in some of the larger cities such as Durham, Greenville, High Point, and Rocky Mountain. The majority of heroin found in North Carolina is transported to North Carolina from New York, Philadelphia, or Baltimore.[8]

Methamphetamine

According to the DEA, **methamphetamine** use is increasing in North Carolina. The drug is produced in the state in clandestine laboratories, particularly in and around Greensboro, as well as being imported from California and Arizona.[9]

Club Drugs

Club drugs include a number of illegal drugs that are found at nightclubs and "raves". The three most common club drugs in North Carolina are MDMA (Ecstacy), GHB (gamma hydroxybutyric acid), and LSD. OxyContin use is also on the rise in North Carolina. These drugs are primarily used by high-school and college-aged students; as the DEA points out, there are over 50 four-year colleges and universities in the state, creating a large potential market for club drugs.[10]

THE DEA IN NORTH CAROLINA

The DEA has a district office located in Charlotte, North Carolina. Main areas of responsibility include the cities of Asheville, Charlotte, Greensboro, Raleigh and Wilmington.[11] During 2001, federal agencies seized over 164 kilograms of cocaine, over 3,800 kilograms of marijuana, and 18 kilograms of methamphetamine. In addition, during 2001, the DEA along with state and local authorities seized 33 clandestine methamphetamine laboratories. The DEA's Domestic Cannabis Eradication and Suppression Program resulted in the eradication of almost 90,000 cultivated marijuana plants in North Carolina.[12]

NORTH CAROLINA DRUG TREATMENT COURTS

Drug courts were developed in North Carolina in 1995 with the passage of the North Carolina Drug Treatment Court Act (NCGS Chapter 7A, Article 62). Drug courts are designed as a way to divert drug offenders out of traditional criminal justice prosecution. They handle cases involving offenders whose crimes are related to substance abuse through the use of extensive supervision and treatment. They also attempt to increase the coordination of various agencies and resources available to drug abusers, increase the cost-effectiveness of the programs, and provide the offender with access to a wide variety of programs and resources. According to NCGS §7A-792, the goals of drug treatment court programs include:

(1) To reduce alcoholism and other drug dependencies among adult and juvenile offenders and defendants and among respondents in juvenile petitions for abuse, neglect, or both;

(2) To reduce criminal and delinquent recidivism and the incidence of child abuse and neglect;

(3) To reduce the aclohol-related (*sic*) and other drug-related court workload;

(4) To increase the personal, familial, and societal accountability of adult and juvenile offenders and defendants and respondents in juvenile petitions for abuse, neglect, or both; and

(5) To promote effective interaction and use of resources among criminal and juvenile justice personnel, child protective services personnel, and community agencies.

Currently, only ten counties in North Carolina have drug courts. These are Buncombe, Caswell, Catawba, Craven, Durham, Forsyth, Guilford, Mecklenburg, New Hanover, Orange, Person, Randolph, Wake and Warren counties.[13] As of January 8, 2003, there were a total of 28 drug courts in the state. This figure included nine drug courts that had been in operation for at least two years and twelve that were recently implemented, as well as seven more that were being planned.[14]

To qualify for participation in a drug court program, an individual must meet certain general criteria. The individual must be addicted to a chemical substance, must be willing to volunteer for the program, and must be eligible for a community or intermediate punishment under structured sentencing. In addition, individual drug court programs may have additional specific eligibility requirements. Certain offenders are ineligible for drug court participation. These include offenders who are not addicted to drugs or chemically dependent, any offender who has been classified as a violent offender, drug dealer, or habitual felon, and any offender ineligible for community or intermediate punishment. In addition, each county program may have existing criteria excluding other types of offenders.[15] Offenders referred to the program are put through an intensive screening process. This includes the collection of information about the defendant's prior and current substance use and abuse as well as information about the defendant's criminal history. First offenders are considered for admission into the program but the majority of participants are multiple offenders who have been through traditional treatment programs but are continuing to reappear in the criminal justice system.[16]

North Carolina drug courts emphasize diversion, probation, and community control. The idea is to divert drug offenders from trial by providing alternatives to traditional criminal justice prosecution for drug-related offenses. Drug court programs generally run for one- to- two years. Offenders must attend drug court sessions biweekly and comply with a variety of court-mandated educational, treatment, and rehabilitation requirements. These may include weekly treatment meetings, attendance at weekly 12-step meetings (e.g., Alcoholics Anonymous, Narcotics Anonymous), compliance with random drug tests, regular home and office visits with a probation officer, anger management classes, GED or literacy classes, participation in vocational rehabilitation, and abstinence from alcohol and other drugs.[17]

If a program participant tests negative for drugs and attends the requirement meetings and treatment programs for a prescribed period of time, the treatment plan will be modified by reducing the requirements. Participants are also provided with referrals to various vocational, academic, and health-related programs. To graduate from a drug court program, the participant must have remained drug-free for the previous four- to- six months (as evidenced by clean urine screens), must have successfully completed all treatment phases of the program, must be employed and regularly paying any legal obligations (taxes, child support, etc.), and must not have committed any new crimes while in the program. If participants do not make adequate progress, the judge may require them to participate in a residential treatment program or send them to jail for a period of time. Offenders may leave the drug court program voluntarily or by failing to comply with the rules of the program. For example, an offender who is found to be using drugs or who is charged with a new felony while in the drug court program may be terminated from the program.[18]

The Durham County Drug Treatment Court

There are three drug treatment courts in the 14th judicial district in North Carolina. The **Adult Drug Treatment Court** works with non-violent repeat drug offenders facing a sentence of incarceration. The program began in November 1999.[19] To be eligible for participation in the program, a defendant must meet the following criteria:

1. Eligible clients by offense can be charged with felony possession of a controlled substance and obtaining controlled substance by fraud or forgery, or who are charged with a felony property crime, and defendants with misdemeanor drug and property crimes, including Level 1 and 2 DWI defendants (pre-disposition), or

2. Defendants who are already on probation and their supervision can be modified to allow supervision in the program (post-disposition); and

3. Defendants who are eligible for a community and/or intermediate sanction within the State's Structured Sentencing Guidelines; and

4. Defendants with no convictions for violent felonies or trafficking or sale of a controlled substance; and

5. No habitual felons; and

6. Defendants who voluntarily enter the Program while acknowledging chemical dependency or a history of substance abuse and express a willingness to actively participate in the program; and

7. Defendants who were not in possession of a firearm at the time of arrest (except defendants charged with DWI); and

8. Defendants who have not previously participated in the program; and

9. Defendants who do not have substantial mental health problems that prohibit their productive participation in the DTC Phase Program; and

10. Defendants who are at least 18 years of age and whose primary residence is in Durham County.[20]

The **Durham Youth Treatment Court** (DYTC) focuses on non-violent juvenile offenders who have admitted or been diagnosed as having a substance abuse problem. The program includes three main components. **Judicial supervision** consists of biweekly appearances in the court. The DYTC judge rewards successful progress and sanction program violations such as drug use. The **treatment** component is tailored to the specific needs of the juvenile and includes weekly (or more frequent) meetings between a court-assigned therapist, the juvenile, and his or her family. Treatment activities may include residential, outpatient, or in-home treatment. Finally, the **educational and skills development** component focuses on encouraging the juvenile to meet various educational and vocational goals as well as helping the family as a whole to develop positive life skills.[21]

The DYTC program is divided into four phases, Phase I, Phase II, Phase III, and Aftercare. The restrictions placed on the youth participant decrease as s/he moves through the phases. The aftercare phase of the program follows the youth after s/he has completed the DYTC program and attempts to ensure that when the youth is back in the community s/he continues to maintain the drug- and alcohol-free lifestyle developed during the court program.[22]

The **Durham Family Drug Treatment Court** (FDCT) focuses on parents or guardians who are substance abusers and who, as a result of this, may be losing or have lost custody of their children. Participants are defendants in child protection cases who want to be reunited with their children and who voluntary enter the FDCT program. The program generally lasts 10-15 months and includes three phases. FDCT participants must remain drug- and alcohol-free during the program and must participate in various treatment activities, such as attendance at weekly 12-step meetings and regular counseling. Participants must also obtain stable employment and housing before they may graduate from the program.[21] The FDCT is a new program; the first session of the court took place on May 30, 2002.[23]

NOTES

1. Office of National Drug Control Policy, Drug Policy Information Clearinghouse (January, 2003). *State of North Carolina: Profile of Drug Indicators*.
    (http://www.whitehousedrugpolicy.gov/statelocal/nc/nc.pdf)
2. Crime in North Carolina 2001 website (http://sbi2.jus.state.nc.us/crp/public/2001/2001.htm)
3. Centers for Disease Control and Prevention, Youth 2001 Online
    (http://www.cdc.gov/nccdphp/dash/yrbs/2001/youth01online.htm)
4. DEA Fact Sheet: *North Carolina* (http://www.usdoj.gov/dea/pubs/states/northcarolina.html)
5. North Carolina State Highway Patrol home page: Statistics
    (http://www.ncshp.org/stats1.html)
6. DEA Fact Sheet: *North Carolina, op. cit.*
7. North Carolina State Highway Patrol home page: Statistics, *op. cit.*
8. DEA Fact Sheet: *North Carolina, op. cit.*
9. *Ibid*
10. *Ibid*
11. *Ibid*
12. ONDCP (Jan., 2003), *op. cit.*
13. The North Carolina Court System home page (http://www.nccourts.org/Default.asp)
14. ONDCP (Jan., 2003), *op. cit.*
15. North Carolina Court System home page, *op. cit.*
16. North Carolina Drug Treatment courts home page (http://www.aoc.state.nc.us/www/dtc)
17. North Carolina Court System home page, *op. cit.*
18. *Ibid*
19. Durham Drug Treatment Court Newsletter, v.1, #1, February 2003
20. Durham County Adult Drug Treatment Court
    (http://www.nccourts.org/County/Durham/Programs/Drug/Adult.asp)
21. Durham County Youth Treatment Court
    (http://www.nccourts.org/County/Durham/Programs/Drug/Youth.asp)
22. Durham County Family Drug Treatment Court
    (http://www.nccourts.org/County/Durham/Programs/Drug/Family.asp)
23. Durham Drug Treatment Court Newsletter, v.1, #1, February 2003

APPENDIX

WEB SITES OF INTEREST

There is a wealth of information on North Carolina and the North Carolina criminal justice system available on the world wide web. Below are a selection of web sites that may be of interest to students.

GENERAL NORTH CAROLINA WEB SITES

http://www.ncgov.com/
> The official home page of the State of North Carolina. It provides a variety of information services for citizens regarding North Carolina history, government, and much more.

http://statelibrary.dcr.state.nc.us/nc/cover.htm
> The home page of the North Carolina Encyclopedia, an online encyclopedia developed by the State Library of North Carolina.

http://www.ncleg.net/homePage.pl
> The official home page of the General Assembly of North Carolina. It includes links to both the Senate and the House of Representatives.

http://www.jus.state.nc.us/
> The home page of the North Carolina Office of the Attorney General.

http://sdc.state.nc.us/
> The home page of the North Carolina State Data Center, which provides census information about the state.

http://www.cjin.jus.state.nc.us/
> The home page of the North Carolina Criminal Justice Information Network.

http://www.nccrimecontrol.org/
> The home page of the North Carolina Department of Crime Control and Public Safety.

LEGAL INFORMATION

http://www.ncleg.net/Legislation/constitution/ncconstitution.html
> This link provides access to the North Carolina State Constitution. You can access the Constitution in HTML, PDF, text, or Microsoft Word formats.

http://www.ncleg.net/gascripts/Statutes/statutestoc.pl
>This link provides access to the North Carolina General Statutes. You can search the statutes by keyword for the specific subject of interest.

POLICE IN NORTH CAROLINA

http://www.ncshp.org/DEFAULT.HTM
>The home page of the North Carolina State Highway Patrol.

http://www.charmeck.nc.us/Departments/Police/Home.htm
>The home page of the Charlotte-Mecklenburg Police Department.

http://www.durhampolice.com/
>The home page of the Durham Police Department.

http://www.charmeck.org/Departments/MCSO/Home.htm
>The home page of the Mecklenburg County Sheriff's Office.

http://www.jus.state.nc.us/otsmain/CJWeb/CJIndex.htm
>The home page of the North Carolina Criminal Justice Education and Training Standards Commission.

http://www.jus.state.nc.us/otsmain/sheriffs/index.htm
>The home page of the North Carolina Sheriff's Education and Training Standards Commission.

http://www.jus.state.nc.us/NCJA/
>The home page of the North Carolina Justice Academy.

THE NORTH CAROLINA COURT SYSTEM

http://www.nccourts.org/Default.asp
>The North Carolina Court System home page.

http://www.ncbar.org/
>The home page of the North Carolina Bar Association.

http://www.aoc.state.nc.us/www/copyright/commissions/sentcom/
>The home page of the North Carolina Sentencing and Policy Advisory Commission

CORRECTIONS IN NORTH CAROLINA

http://www.doc.state.nc.us/
>The home page of the North Carolina Department of Correction.

THE NORTH CAROLINA JUVENILE JUSTICE SYSTEM

http://www.juvjus.state.nc.us/
>The home page of the North Carolina Department of Juvenile Justice and Delinquency Prevention.

DRUGS IN NORTH CAROLINA

http://www.whitehousedrugpolicy.gov/statelocal/nc/index.html
>The Office of National Drug Control Policy provides a large amount of information on drug use statistics and drug prevention efforts in Florida.

http://www.usdoj.gov/dea/pubs/states/northcarolina.html
>The Drug Enforcement Agency has factsheets on every state in the U.S.

http://www.aoc.state.nc.us/www/dtc/description.html
>The home page of the North Carolina Drug Treatment Court Program.